Because We Love Them:

A Handbook For Animal Lovers

BY

ANNA C. BRIGGS

PRESIDENT
THE NATIONAL HUMANE EDUCATION SOCIETY

WITH

CONSTANCE CLARK

Front Cover Photo: Ed Simpson/T.S.I.

TABLE OF CONTENTS

ACKNOWLEDGMENTS

This book would not have been possible without the kind cooperation and information provided by representatives of humane groups across the United States. To name just a few, we extend warmest thanks to the American Humane Association, Defenders of Wildlife, the Humane Society of the United States, the Wildlife Management Institute, the World Society for the Protection of Animals, and the Massachusetts Society for the Prevention of Cruelty to Animals.

Many experts from these groups gave generously of their time and knowledge. Thanks to them, this book deals with the broadest possible array of issues regarding how we treat animals in America. From dogs and cats to mice, birds, and elephants, animals are seen in all the ways they "serve" humans: as objects of affection, education, research, and testing; as sources of food and clothing; and as contestants in sporting activities.

Because of the wide participation from humane groups, we have been able to make this book a comprehensive look at the way we treat animals—and how we need to alter our behavior to better meet *their* needs and respect *their* rights. This book is an illustration of the maxim that there is strength in numbers: By pooling our resources, humane groups not only can produce more persuasive arguments for their causes, they also stand to persuade more people to the fact that animals deserve our love, our respect, and our thoughtful stewardship.

Anna C. Briggs
Leesburg, Virginia
January 1994

PREFACE:
ON A PERSONAL NOTE

Early on in my life, I learned an important lesson. I'm not sure exactly where I learned it, or who taught it to me, but I was so impressed by its wisdom and hope that I have never swerved from practicing it since.

Many years later, after decades of putting it into practice in my life, I learned that this lesson was encapsulated in the Talmud, the Jewish commentaries on the Old Testament. There, it is written: "He who saves a single life saves the entire world."

Of course, the principle speaks primarily to helping other human beings in need or distress. It applies to those who rescue the victims of natural disasters, or those who saved Jews from the gas chambers under the brutal Nazi regime. Even though many people are savagely killed for no good reason, saving even one life is an important symbol of the sanctity of life for all of God's creatures.

It is our way of speaking out for life, of showing others that *every* life is precious and deserves to be saved.

In my life, I have taken this motto one step further. For me, it's important to extend this sentiment toward animals — those poor, defenseless creatures who, because they cannot speak for themselves, so often are abused, mistreated, and killed. Believe me, this is not sentimentalism, but a reasoned, logical position.

Since I was 13 years old, I grew up around animals. I've had dogs, cats, and other creatures in my life since those formative years. And I have never been able to bear to watch an animal suffer, particularly at the hands of human beings who know better. To see a wretched, abandoned pet by the side of the highway, or a bruised and beaten dog or cat struggling to survive—these are things that make me ill inside.

I believe we have a responsibility to these creatures to give them a decent life: food, water, a home, and respect for their lives. That's not a lot, but for *millions* of animals in the United States alone it means the difference between life and death.

Just think about it: if more people would follow this rule in their life, more lives would be saved, whether it's the lives of human beings or animals. For example, if we could get *ten million* Americans to adopt a pet from their local animal shelter in the coming year, not one single animal would have to be put to sleep for lack of space to "hold" them.

You might say that I'm being wildly optimistic, but my point still stands. It starts with *you*, with one person doing good, setting the example and showing the way for others to follow. That's the most powerful statement you and I can make in this world where the loss of a life often seems to make so little difference.

Perhaps one of the easiest ways we can show our humanity is by being proper stewards of the creatures God put on this earth. If we can each take good care of the puppies and kittens, dogs and cats and other animals in our homes, we will already be making significant inroads on the terrible problem of inhumane treatment of animals.

Here are some simple tasks all of us can and should contribute:

- Take the time to have your animals spayed or neutered, so they won't breed unwanted offspring.
- Make sure your pets are well fed and well cared for.
- Make it a priority to watch out for the pets in your neighborhood—if one is lost, help recover it; if another seems like it is being abused, take steps to see that it stops, and so on.

Most dogs and cats have little defense in the face of human cruelty. They are routinely tortured, maimed, killed, and experimented on for a variety of "good" and not-so-good reasons. And, as you will learn in the pages of this book, even the so-called "good" reasons don't bear up under close scrutiny. Although we as human beings have choices as to how to act, with regard to animals our range of choices should be limited to those actions which promote the life and health of the creatures now under our care.

With this principle in mind—that if you save one life, you've saved the world—I hope you will learn many things about how we as a society deal with our animal populations, as well as some of the antidotes to our often terrible, neglectful behavior. The responsibility to change is ours, and I hope you will join me in shouldering this responsibility.

CHAPTER I

An Animal Lover's
Ten Commandments

Do animals have rights?
Should they have the same rights as humans?
Should these rights extend to every animal?

We speak of human beings having "rights," or privileges recognized by societies and governments for such practices as speech, association, reproduction, and employment. To understand just how important rights are, it has been observed that, where rights have been denied or curtailed, social unrest and/or political instability usually result.

A growing number of people and governments now accept that animals, too, have certain basic rights: the right to eat, to make a home for themselves, to propagate their species, and to move from place to place (such as to migrate).

But where do we get such notions—and how do we apply them not only to human beings, but to all forms of life?

I. *Origin and Nature of Rights and Ethics*

Human rights are the recognition by society that people should be granted due justice, and their need for proper nutrition, employment, homes, and reproduction should be respected. Rights can be spelled out in laws or constitutions, or they can be respected from a sense of tradition alone.

1

Ethics refers to the obligation each person has to behave justly toward other people. This obligation is also spelled out in laws, but often is based on traditional notions of what is right and wrong.

Humans are unique in the Animal Kingdom in that they set standards for themselves in their treatment of other animals. The respect for animals' rights (related to the satisfaction of basic needs) and the ethical behavior towards animals are set according to rules of what is moral and immoral in human behavior toward other animals.

Now, even though we live in an advanced civilization, there are still people who deny rights to animals and who refuse to be held to ethical standards in their behavior toward animals. These callous persons contrast sharply with the many who freely and willingly allow humane concerns as rights, and allow ethics to govern human-animal relations.

II. *Why People Respect Ethics and Rights*

Since the beginnings of civilization, people have held the belief that human behavior must be regulated, so that people and other animals are treated justly. In biblical times and in the writings of the philosophers, a system of thought was considered incomplete, even immoral, if proper recognition was not given to ethical concerns.

Fortunately for *all* creatures, today we have returned to this important notion. To take a modern example, North Carolina State University Professor Tom Regan predicts that a new, peaceful revolution is building throughout much of the world, in which greater numbers of humans have accepted and adjusted their beliefs and behavior to meet certain ethical standards. Professor Regan calls this modern-day movement the "thee" generation, as distinct from the "me" generation.

The "thee" generation, according to Professor Regan, calls on critical biblical passages as a foundation for the belief that all creatures are endowed with rights. This means a rejection of humanism, a school of thought which has traditionally placed humans above and outside the realm of nature rather than as an equal member in it.

According to Professor Regan, the "me" generation has been concerned mainly with accumulation; through possessions, these people try to show they are above the rest of the world. The "me" generation advocates reject animal rights and behave in selfish, narrow ways toward other humans and creatures. They are not necessarily immoral, but they are misguided because they have been improperly educated.

The "thee" generation, Professor Regan insists, believes strongly in the oneness and equality of life. Species have evolved gradually during the past billion years, but this evolution has not resulted in putting humans on a pedestal above other forms of life. If evolution has anything to teach us, it is that all living beings have been essential to the development of all others. Of course, many creatures and plants have passed out of existence at certain times, but this does not imply that they were "inferior" and unnecessary to the evolution of life. All life forms are intimately and profoundly interconnected.

So that the "thee" generation can behave morally, followers ask themselves: "What can I do for animals?" "What can I do for the environment?" "What can I do for peace and nonviolence?"—not "What will these things do for me?"

Through these questions, the "thee" generation is striving to achieve a peaceful revolution in the thoughts, attitudes, and behavior of humans. Followers say this revolution is on the horizon and will bring with it fundamental changes in society's institutions, laws, and human behavior. The centerpiece of these changes will relate to the rights and ethics for humans and other animals.

According to Professor Regan, this revolution is underway. The world-wide movement toward democracy and the growing recognition and respect for humans and other animal rights are prime indicators. By contrast, the "me" generation is losing its influence, largely because their beliefs and behavior are founded on the shifting sands of greed.

Professor Regan believes this revolution will more profoundly change society than the violent revolutions of the past, because the basic beliefs of societies reflected in its laws, institutions, and the behavior of people will be drastically altered. However, the changes will be peaceful and will proceed through persuasion and example: more and more individuals will come to believe in and live by nonviolent, ethical standards.

The impact of this revolution will be seen in the answers people find when they ask themselves, "What are we and other animals?" "What do we believe?" and "What should our behavior toward humans and creatures be?" People are increasingly demanding that science serve the needs of this new ethic.

Many idealistic persons are in the "thee" movement because they are seeking to fulfill the existence and achievements of all beings. Now, of course, most creatures cannot speak for themselves. Nor can the crops, the trees, the soils, the rivers and lakes, the oceans, and the atmosphere of our world, which must nevertheless be preserved and protected for future generations. But human beings can, should, and will speak on behalf of their mute co-creatures.

Although kindness and other charitable acts of humans are essential and good, the basic tenet of the "thee" movement is justice for all people and other animals.

But not all people or nations accept these rights for animals. Those of us who accept animal rights need to learn why others deny these rights to creatures—and why these arguments are wrong.

III. *Why People Reject Rights and Ethical Behavior for Animals*

If there is a common denominator in the views of persons who reject rights and ethical treatment for animals, it is that they seem to have vested interests; all of these people make a living in part through the unethical treatment of animals.

The prime offenders include:

• Biomedical researchers, who insist that unrestricted use of live creatures is essential to progress in science and medicine;

• Hunters and trappers who seek free use of animals for recreation and special products such as fur;

• Educators who use live animals in instruction in secondary schools and institutions of higher learning;

• Zoos and circuses that keep live creatures in cages for viewing by the public; and

• Farmers who raise animals to provide food for humans.

In these and other cases, certain persons view live animals primarily or exclusively as a means for acquiring a livelihood.

In my more than sixty years' experience in the animal rights movement, I have come across ten basic statements espoused by the antagonists of believers of animal rights. I offer these negative statements as prime examples of "me" generation thinking and will refute these claims in the pages that follow:

1. *They* say that animal rights advocates equate animals and humans, when, in fact, we acknowledge that humans and other animals differ greatly.

2. *They* say we view humans and animals as having the same rights. Of course, this is absurd. Chickens cannot

exercise the right to vote, nor could pigs take advantage
of the right to higher education.

3. *They* argue that, if animals have rights, then so do
vegetables, which is also absurd.

4. *They* argue that it is impossible to draw the line
between animals that deserve rights and those that don't.
If primates and rodents have rights, then so should slugs
and amoebas.

5. *They* admit that some animals experience pain;
however, since animals lack a unified psychological
identity, what we call a "personality," they do not earn
the right to be treated with respect. Therefore, they can
be used in any way humans choose.

6. *They* claim that, since animals don't respect the
rights of humans, people don't have an obligation to
respect the rights of animals.

7. *They* argue that God gave humans dominion over
the animals, so we can do anything we want with them—
including eating their flesh and wearing their pelts.

8. *They* say only humans have immortal souls, so
people can treat other creatures in any manner they see
fit. To kill an animal is not to kill a soul, according to
them.

9. *They* argue that, if humans did not control animal
populations by killing them for food and other products,
animals would eventually overrun our homes, streets, and
cities.

10. *They* feel there are many more pressing issues
than animal rights. People should give more attention to
world hunger and child abuse, to apartheid and illicit
drugs, to violence against women and the plight of the
homeless—than to the rights of animals.

Some specific arguments used to legitimize humans'
vested interests in the mistreatment of animals go as
follows:

Hunters pay taxes on guns and ammunition. They argue that, by paying such taxes, they are given the right to shoot and trap animals for sport, food, and such products as pelts and hides for garments. Many local, state, and national governments endorse the interests of hunters through laws and regulations.

Biomedical researchers claim that many advances in medicine and science have resulted through investigations using animals. These same researchers often argue that advances that will alleviate the suffering of humans can occur only if they are allowed free, unlimited use of animals. There is no place in their reasoning for the idea that other creatures should also have the right to live free from pain and torture.

Farmers, ranchers, and the institutions marketing their products insist that animals are needed for their flesh and other byproducts. Because of their interest in preserving their own business, they say the supply of food and clothing would be inadequate to meet human demand if animals were not reared for their end products.

Zoo and circus operators—even *educators*—insist they have the right to use creatures for their own purposes and profit; they have successfully persuaded governments at all levels to guarantee and regulate these pursuits through laws.

People often invoke the argument that, since humans have depended on animals for a variety of selfish uses since prehistoric times, we, too, have the right to continue such a tradition. According to this argument, "nature" has endowed humans with rights but did not extend the privilege to animals.

IV. *Why People Recognize Animal Rights*

Today, more and more people insist that animals have basic rights similar to those of humans. Like humans, animals suffer pain—and they should enjoy the right, wherever possible, to be spared pain at the hands of humans. In the spirit of the "thee" generation, animal rights advocates believe humans have the capacity, and the distinct privilege, to carry out a higher good. This is the basis for the humane treatment of animals.

Some people advocate that we should not eat animal flesh. They argue that a strictly vegetarian diet is equal and even superior to a menu prescribing animal flesh products. These same people usually maintain that it is cruel and unnecessary to use animal hides and pelts for garments and decoration.

And biomedical research would *not* suffer if experimenters could no longer use animals. Many sound scientific advances have resulted from experiments with tissue cultures and experimental models rather than live animals—advances like the discovery of the cause of the AIDS virus, the development of penicillin and antibiotics, X-ray and CAT-scan machines, and the beneficial properties of vitamins and minerals. It is likely that future advances would not require research "guinea pigs" either.

Veterinarians and doctors of human medicine in growing numbers are protesting against laboratory experiments performed on live animals. They have succeeded in persuading funding groups and government agencies to stop supplying funds in support of such cruel research.

Animal rights advocates also argue that hunting is not really a sport at all, because it requires the use of guns. These same advocates maintain that animals have the right to live in peace and freedom, and if people insist on viewing them, they can do so in the creatures' natural homes (rather than in the unnatural environments of zoos and circuses), using cameras instead of guns.

V. The "Ten Commandments" of The National Humane Education Society

Our Society is in substantial agreement with animal rights advocates. The Society's policy rests on a number of sound ethical principles, in sharp contrast to the ten objections of those who do not believe in animal rights:

1. Animals have as much of a right to live as humans. They also deserve to procreate and propagate their species as part of the natural law. Where overpopulation threatens their quality of life and stimulates suffering and cruelty for them, steps such as spaying and neutering are necessary and appropriate birth control measures.

Animal rights advocates are not saying that all living beings are equal in all ways. Of course, dogs and cats are incapable of learning calculus, and pigs and cows are not equipped to enjoy poetry. But like humans, many creatures have a psychological makeup which must be respected.

2. People share many, if not all, basic moral rights with many creatures. Even though chickens can't vote and pigs can't enroll in higher education, they must be treated justly. And all are entitled to live in relative peace and freedom.

A consequence of this idea is that there are few, if any, valid reasons for killing live animals for sport. Guns and traps prevent animals from offering any resistance to their capture, so there is no real "sport" involved. Hunting is simply being cruel to animals, thinly disguised as play.

3. Vegetables don't deserve the same basic rights as animals, because plants lack anything resembling a brain and a nervous system. Animals, on the other hand, do have brains and well-developed nervous systems, and therefore deserve to be treated on a different plane from plants.

One way in which we observe the difference is in the human diet. Animal flesh is not a prerequisite for a healthy diet. On the other hand, fruits and vegetables are excellent sources of nutrients and proteins, low in cholesterol, full of fiber and healthy bulk, and fulfill the requirements of a healthy lifestyle. We do no harm in eating fruits and vegetables; we do do harm when we kill animals to eat their flesh.

4. Even though we cannot draw a precise line between creatures that have a psychological makeup and those that do not, sound scientific methods tell us that primates and rodents fall to one side, whereas slugs and amoebas are on the other.

So, when we kill animals such as foxes, muskrats, and minks, we destroy their souls as well. Strictly speaking, this is an unnecessary form of killing. The use of hides and pelts is not needed for garments. Attractive, warm, and far less costly garments can be made from synthetic and vegetable fibers.

5. Some creatures experience pain even though they lack a unified psychological identity. It is ethically wrong to cause pain to these animals if this pain is unnecessary, regardless of whether the creatures are monkeys or oysters.

Advances in medicine today do not require the use of animals in research. Disease prevention and the use of tissue cultures and computer models are equal to the task and are being used by a growing number of investigators at the forefront of medicine and science. So, giving pain to animals in this context is completely unjustified.

6. It is wrong to believe that, just because other animals don't understand or respect human rights, people don't have to respect the rights of creatures. Humans have special capacities to help them realize their moral duty with regard to other animals. Put in plain English, we as humans know better—in a way, it's similar to what adults

say to their children who imitate bad behavior: "You should know better than to...!"

It's important to give children the right message from the start. One example of this is the biology-classroom dissection of frogs, rabbits, and other creatures, which is not really necessary for instruction. Dummies can be assembled and then taken apart to teach students about the organs of living creatures. And later on, in advancing scientific and medical education at the university level, human cadavers have proven to be the most effective tools.

7. In giving humans dominion over other creatures, God did not intend for us to abuse animals. Careful study of Scripture reveals that dominion means unselfish guardianship, not selfish, cruel, or wanton power. Humans must be as loving toward all creatures as God was in creating them.

In this sense, the use of animals in product safety testing is patently misguided and unwarranted. How animals respond to radiation, irritable products, and even surgery are not comparable to responses in humans. Humans are not biologically the same as lower animals; for product testing to be reliably effective, researchers must find human volunteers who would willingly undergo testing.

8. Even if it is accepted that other animals lack an immortal soul, this does not decrease our obligation to respect the rights of creatures. Animals deserve a full life just as humans do, regardless of whether one has been promised immortality after death.

9. Concerning human control of animal populations, people already contribute to potential population problems by rearing billions of creatures for food. If humans stopped breeding excess animals, there would be far fewer creatures alive. Control of wild creatures is unnecessary because nature has built-in population controls.

As far as pets and domestic animals go, sterilizing them is a humane, pro-active approach to preventing overpopulation.

10. As to other pressing problems, including world hunger, creatures warrant our attention along with grappling with the other pressing problems. It should not be a question of "either/or" but of simultaneously addressing *all* critical problems.

If there is one idea you should have after reading this book, it is that the humane treatment of animals is a pressing issue, one which has gotten too far out of control and which now requires severe, strong measures.

I have always tried to live my life and guide my behavior by the Scriptures, and Professor Regan's views on the "thee" generation seem to me to be in full accord with Scriptural teaching and example. Now, even though it may not be explicitly stated in the Bible, I find the ethical path outlined in the Scripture does indeed hold true for how we are to treat animals.

Christ prophesied a revolution in people's thinking and behavior. The social revolution now building in the world is a consequence of what Christ foresaw—a realm where all humans and all animals could live peaceably together and respect one another's lives and habitats.

VI. *Conclusion*

People and groups who argue against animals having rights usually do so for personal self-interest. Whether they are the so-called sportsmen, medical and scientific investigators, product safety researchers, or educators, their use of live animals is not essential to the public good.

Those who argue for animal rights do so from a sense of humane ethics. "Lower" animals have the same basic rights as humans to eat, grow, live in safe havens, and rear their young. This mature ethic is winning over many converts who now understand the unethical nature of many cruel, unnecessary practices using live animals.

The National Humane Education Society sees a new pattern emerging in human beliefs, attitudes, and actions. It is true that other animals cannot speak, but we can speak for them. We have that capability—and that responsibility—with regard to the creatures under our care. Because people have the ability to distinguish right from wrong, humans are obliged to make full use of these traits to assure the just treatment of creatures so they remain part of the heritage we pass down to future generations of creatures, human and otherwise.

In the chapters that follow, you will see how the "Ten Commandments" apply to our behavior and attitudes toward animals.

CHAPTER II

A National Disgrace

What's the best kept secret about violence in America?

Answer: That we routinely kill millions of puppies and kittens, dogs and cats each year.

And the reason it's a "secret" is that, unlike the violence on our city streets, we don't *see* the violence done to these defenseless creatures. They are quietly "put to sleep" in the back rooms of our nation's 1,500 animal shelters.

According to the American Society for the Prevention of Cruelty to Animals (ASPCA), about ten million pet cats and dogs are prematurely put to death in pounds each year. By any reckoning, this immense killing of unwanted and lost pets is shocking. This mass euthanasia, or "mercy killing," has occurred in spite of the fact that many shelters have adopt-a-pet programs. Because there are not enough good people who come forward for these animals, and because housing restrictions prevent many willing people from keeping pets, only 20% of all pets entering the shelters are adopted. The other 80% are euthanized.

Of course, the overabundance of these creatures cheapens the intrinsic value of each animal. One sad result of this overpopulation is that some people resort to cruel methods of disposal, such as abandoning pets in the wild or alongside roadways. Practices such as drowning unwanted kittens and puppies are still all too common.

You see, there are simply too many cats and dogs born each year to find good homes for. Another part of the problem is that pet owners too often refuse or fail to have their pets sterilized. Owners' lack of care regarding birth control contributes to the tremendous over-population of cats and dogs.

Pet owners have a responsibility to care for the pets under their roof. Communities, municipalities, and states need to find solutions to the animal overpopulation problem. Each and every human being needs to lend a hand in providing for the welfare of existing animals—not just house pets, but also the millions of unwanted, abandoned animals. If we don't do something, who will?

Animal overpopulation is not a problem that will take care of itself with time, either. Every hour, 450 humans are born in the United States, compared to 3,000 puppies and kittens! Simple arithmetic will tell you that, even if every new human being were to accept a pet, a tremendous surplus would still result. If you consider that nearly 60% of American households now have pets, the numbers—and the problem—are still way out of control.

I. *The Dilemmas of Shelters*

It's not the fault of animal shelter workers—they're just the ones who have to deal with the consequences of our imprudent behavior toward dogs and cats.

People who work in animal shelters get no pleasure from destroying animals. They wish they could care for each lost or abandoned creature until a good home was found, but the sheer burden of the numbers forces them to dispose of creatures in a short time—usually after about ten days. Since staff members, like the rest of us, feel that life is precious, they suffer when circumstances force them to end life for these poor creatures. It is indeed a sad fact of life, but until we succeed in controlling births, which is easily within our means and abilities, the tragedy will persist.

The cost of running large shelters as a consequence of overpopulation is also a factor contributing to the problem. Our country spends more than $300 million annually for animal welfare and control, including running shelters and control agencies, but even this amount of money has not solved the pet problem. Again, we need more effective controls on unwanted births.

There is no law in the United States regulating how shelters must be run. Many shelters, however, set their own, relatively high standards of feeding, housing, and destroying unwanted creatures that can no longer be cared for in the most humane way possible.

But shelters cannot guarantee humane treatment. Often, instead of being put to sleep, unwanted animals are claimed by research laboratories, where they are subjected to a succession of barbarous experiments. It's hard to tell which fate is worse—a quick death or a reprieve so that the creature's body can be poked, prodded, drugged, and subjected to horrors which I cannot bring myself to describe!

II. *Pound Seizures—A Terrible Way To Live*

"Pound seizure" refers to the taking of cats and dogs from shelters and pounds to serve as models in biomedical research. This practice goes back many decades, mostly in the form of small-scale local projects; however, it became widespread after World War II, as funding for biomedical research skyrocketed. Today, shelters usually object to this practice, even though a few states have laws requiring it.

Some scientists say there is no reason not to use shelter animals for experimental purposes. After all, they argue, the animals were lost or abandoned and will most likely wind up being euthanized in shelters and pounds to make room for the heavy influx of more unwanted pets.

As President of the National Humane Education Society, I find this practice to be ethically bad and scientifically invalid. Animals who have already bonded to people as pets depend on humans for care. Sentencing them to the torture in labs is morally reprehensible. As far as scientific validity goes, I feel that shelter animals are not even appropriate for scientific use, since the animals' histories are not fully known by the researchers, as they would be for animals bred specifically for this purpose. Nothing is known about the shelter creatures' origins, health conditions, and age.

The National Humane Education Society favors a total ban on *any* use of *any* animal for biomedical research. We favor the development of alternative models for the investigations. In the absence of a total ban, the Society favors at the very least making it impossible for shelters and pounds to allow their animals to serve as guinea pigs in research labs.

Martha Armstrong, speaking on behalf of the Massachusetts Society for the Prevention of Cruelty to Animals, points out that 12 states (including Massachusetts) already ban such use. On the other hand, 6 states mandate or approve of the practice, and 32 others leave it open as an option to be exercised by specific labs and researchers. But Ms. Armstrong adds, "The 1983 Massachusetts bill passed by the State Legislature and approved by the Governor bans the practice totally. Labs may not use in-state public or private shelter or pound animals, and the ban extends to out-of-state animals."

According to Ms. Armstrong, "This ban has not collapsed biomedical research, nor has it run up costs. Our state continues as a leading jurisdiction with biomedical labs. We therefore believe the Massachusetts law is a model for the other states to adapt to their jurisdictions."

Where does the public at large stand on this issue? Two nationwide surveys—the Nelson Rees survey conducted in 1987 and the National Enquirer survey in 1988—found that an overwhelming majority of pet owners are against allowing pets to be sent to research labs. Indeed, the first survey found that 95% percent of those polled objected to the practice, while the second survey registered 89% opposed.

On a national level, measures have already been taken to see that pound animals are not used for biomedical research. The National Institutes of Health have a policy barring shelter animals from all in-house research.

New York State's Metcalf-Hatch Bill, passed in 1953, is a good example of the strong negative effects a law permitting pound seizure can have. Until the passage of this ill-conceived legislation, the New York City-based American Society for the Prevention of Cruelty to Animals had been doing an outstanding job handling the thousands of stray and unwanted animals. Under the Metcalf-Hatch Act, however, New Yorkers no longer sent their own or stray animals to local shelters, fearing that the pets would wind up in labs, so many cats and dogs became strays.

In this period of great distress, Alice Morgan Wright, co-founder of the National Humane Education Society, was contacted at her home in Albany and begged to do something about the desperate situation. Ms. Wright turned the problem over to me, since I was then director of activities at the Peace Plantation shelter in Sterling, Virginia, a facility that didn't turn stray animals over to the labs.

I went to Brooklyn and was astonished by the number of strays that Ms. Wright had been feeding daily for many months. She was adamant about not turning any of the animals over to a Brooklyn shelter or pound, because she feared they would wind up in labs. While I went about my work of trapping the cats to take back to Peace Plantation, other people told me they would rather see the creatures eke out an existence as strays than see them turned over to local shelters to be forwarded to labs.

That was the first of my many trips to New York City to rescue strays. Eventually, I had more of these animals at Peace Plantation than from any other area, all because of the dreaded Metcalf-Hatch Bill.

In the meantime, Ms. Wright and other diligent volunteers worked hard to get the state law repealed. After a number of years, they were able to do so. The public once again could put their trust in shelters, which were no longer required to help scientists carry out their gruesome experiments.

What is being done today to mitigate the tragedy of too many cats and dogs—and how can you get involved?

III. *Some Creative Solutions*

We need legislation in all local jurisdictions mandating the sterilization of cats and dogs to prevent unwanted births. A recently passed New Jersey law is a good prototype for other state laws: It provides funds to subsidize spaying and neutering of all cats and dogs adopted from shelters and pounds. Unfortunately, the law does not apply to pets acquired from pet stores or other owners, but it is a step in the right direction.

Some shelters have started a spay/neuter clinic in their own buildings with a visiting veterinarian who schedules specific times for free alterings. Donations for this purpose are put in donation boxes by the general public who visit the shelters. Also, some shelters such as Peace Plantation, run by The National Humane Education Society, have their own spay/neuter clinics.

The Los Angeles city government has adopted legislation that goes even further. It provides for subsidizing spaying and neutering of all cats and dogs, so that the cost to owners is less than $25 per pet. This program has had considerable success in preventing unwanted births: since the legislation was passed, the number of pets given to shelters has gone down by one-third. Officials are convinced this reduction is due to effective controls on the soaring population of cats and dogs.

Since many owners adopt pets without thinking how they will take care of them, widespread education is needed to teach owner responsibility, so they can care for the creatures humanely and not end up abandoning or turning them over to shelters. If communities can also establish cooperative sterilization programs with veterinarians, it would make a difference to owners who otherwise couldn't afford the service.

With adoption rates at shelters now running at less than 20%, we need to increase the adoption of shelter animals. Again, education—getting the word out about the problem of overpopulation and what people can do to help—will help increase the adoption rate. The local press often helps by publishing stories and pictures of animals in need of adoption.

Perhaps we need to rethink the problem as well, so that we might come up with more creative solutions. Considering that cats and dogs have a highly beneficial effect on the health and happiness of humans, there ought to be a way to promote this fact in order to find homes for more unwanted animals. We have evidence from hospitals, clinics, nursing homes, and residences that pets actually help make life more enjoyable for the elderly, the lonely, and the sick.

For example, a Chicago clinic introduced a "puppy hour" before it was time to give the elderly patients their medication. The puppies fussed over the patients so much that these people forgot their dislike of having to take medicine. The result was dramatic, yet predictable: patients willingly took their medication and requested that the puppies visit every day. Some patients' depressive states improved to such a degree that they required less medication—all because of a few puppies!

I could cite you many examples of kittens and puppies, grown cats and dogs who lavish attention and love on people in all sorts of conditions. The elderly, whose children have grown up and who now find themselves alone, are especially in need of such affection. Each cat and dog placed with an elderly person means that a life is saved—and another one is enriched! Matching pets with people is therefore essential to the well-being of both the animal *and* the human being.

Another problem faced in adopting pets relates to living restrictions. In many apartment buildings, tenants are prohibited from having pets. This restriction is often written into their leases, so tenants risk eviction if they take in an animal.

It is my opinion that this is a thoroughly misguided restriction. Most pets do not harm properties or cause a nuisance to other residents. I see no reason why pets should not be welcomed in every apartment building, particularly since having pets makes many tenants more content and, hence, potentially less troublesome to building owners and managers. Since lonely people often respond positively to the steady affection of cats and dogs, they deserve the chance to receive such gratification. Pets also can give people living alone a sense of security; many are afraid to open their doors to strangers, but they would feel more secure with a dog around.

We also need more "no-kill" shelters in the United States like Peace Plantation, the National Humane Education Society's refuge for unwanted animals. At Peace Plantation, animals are kept for as long as it takes to find them good homes. Space limitations and the overwhelming number of animals taken in force public shelters to destroy many creatures within ten days. If we could open more shelters, there would be room for more abandoned and lost puppies and kittens. Perhaps fewer of them would have to die untimely deaths.

Peace Plantation is one of a growing number of sanctuaries that resist euthanasia and work hard to find good homes for the creatures brought to them. But the staggering size of the over-population means that shelters cannot take care of the problem by themselves.

The National Humane Education Society firmly believes that the ultimate answer to the tragic overabundance of cats and dogs in our society is to exert population controls, such as the sterilization of pets before they reach breeding age. Citizens and animal-rights groups must lobby for legislation in each local jurisdiction to require spaying and neutering.

The Society recognizes the importance of educational programs to teach pet responsibility to potential and actual owners of cats and dogs. More such programs need to be created. The biggest shame in all of this is that, all too often, puppies and kittens are brought into a home and then abandoned—either taken to a shelter or literally dumped on the side of a highway or in a park—simply because the owners find they or their children cannot take care of their pets. Education is our only hope of breaking such a cruel, avoidable cycle of abandonment.

CHAPTER III

Practicing On Pets

You've no doubt heard the stories of children trying to light the tail of a cat with a match, pulling them by the tail or a paw, or other such abusive behavior.

And you've probably been appalled to see their parents discussing these events and laughing—as though this were just the pranksterish behavior of their precious tots.

So why should we be concerned when we see children abusing animals?

As far back as the 13th century, during the era of the great theologian Thomas Aquinas, it was suspected that the cruel treatment of animals by children was related to the subsequent cruelty of adult humans toward one another. Practically speaking, though, even when this link is acknowledged, it is usually overlooked by most parents, who tend to believe their children's behavior is merely a phase that the children will outgrow.

Today, we cannot condone such an oversight. With advances in psychology, we can be far more alert to childhood trends and the characteristics or "habits" they portend; psychologists and other medical specialists can provide remedies that correct this early, cruel behavior before it becomes potentially dangerous to other humans.

Of course, it is also important to put an end to such behavior on its own terms, because animals suffer from the abuse they receive from children—whether it is inflicted consciously or not. As parents, we have a responsibility to instill in our young a love and respect for animal life as well. True affection toward animals will fuel a sense of wonder and respect for all forms of life.

I. *Scope of the Problem*

Many researchers in the United States have found strong links between children who mistreat animals and adults who are violent toward other human beings. It seems that, to an alarming degree, men and women who beat, rape, and kill others were once children who displayed cruel behavior toward animals.

For example, from their investigations in the 1970s and 1980s, Doctors Alan Felthous and Stephen Kellert concluded the following:

• Violence against pets may be an indicator of other forms of family violence.

• Physical abuse of a child sometimes results in the youngster abusing animals and other children; this behavior has been known to persist into adulthood.

• Children who act aggressively toward animals often become adults responsible for abuse, rape, and killing of humans.

• Aggression among adult criminals often has a history of early family abuse and childhood cruelty toward animals.

Such findings—and the fact that the public seemed for the most part unaware of them—led the American Humane Association (AHA) to convene conferences in 1991 and 1992, so that leading researchers could report on the results of their investigations into this important link. The AHA is a national organization working to protect both children and animals.

At the conferences, experts shared their insights and knowledge of the link between children abusing animals and adult criminal behavior, so the public could become more informed about this unfortunate linkage. These meetings were particularly helpful in getting the word out to other specialists, parents, and the criminal justice system. A commitment was made to bring the message home to school administrators, teachers, and other authorities dealing with children.

Most important, however, was that an overwhelming consensus of opinion was formed at the conferences that, indeed, there is a strong connection between cruelty toward animals in childhood and violence toward humans in adulthood.

It is easiest to grasp this link in the examples of specific criminals. For example:

• Jeffrey Dahmer, who killed and dismembered 17 men, reportedly as a child was fond of impaling frogs and staking cats to trees in his backyard.

• David Berkowitz, New York City's "Son of Sam" murderer, was said to have killed a number of dogs in his youth.

• Brenda Spencer, who fired 40 shots at San Diego school children during their recess, reportedly abused cats and dogs in her youth, including setting their tails on fire.

• Albert DeSalvo, the famed "Boston Strangler," as a youngster liked to trap dogs and cats, place them in orange crates, and shoot arrows through the boxes.

• Carroll Edward Cole, who admitted his guilt in several vicious murders, remembers how he strangled a cat when he was a young child.

Could such brutal crimes against humans have been prevented if dangerous childhood behavior toward animals had been recognized and properly dealt with?

Many investigators feel that early treatment for the aberrant behavior most likely would have led to changes in the personality of the child and prevented him or her from becoming a dangerous criminal as an adult.

In another major study carried out by Doctors Kellert and Felthous in 1987, 152 convicted criminals were interviewed and all were found to have committed acts of cruelty toward animals in childhood. The researchers identified nine motives leading to animal cruelty:

1. Excessive and sometimes cruel physical punishment was used to control or shape the animals' behavior;

2. Animals were punished severely in revenge for their behavior;

3. Violent acts towards the animals resulted from simple prejudice, or a lack of knowledge;

4. Violent aggressive behavior was intended to train the animals to attack other animals or people;

5. Some subjects killed or abused the animals to improve their own aggressive skills or to impress others with their capacity for violence;

6. Cruelty toward the animals was for amusement;

7. Cruelty was sometimes a substitute for striking back at other persons;

8. Aggression against the animals was inflicted to retaliate against authority figures that the person hated or feared; and

9. Desire to inflict suffering or death to the animals resulted out of a sadistic desire for enjoyment.

Police, teachers, social workers, ministers, and other leaders in the community who see children commit such cruelty toward animals should recognize the potential danger if remedial action is not taken immediately. Parents should be encouraged to seek treatment for their children to eradicate the sources of such unhealthy behavior.

The role of the National Humane Education Society in this arena involves publicizing, as widely as possible, the link between children's cruelty to animals and adult violence toward human beings. Through the print and electronic media, the public must be shown that brutal criminal violence will persist until we can successfully treat early childhood violence toward animals.

Let me quote briefly from the 1987 AHA report:

"Violence has many manifestations, but the forces and influences that foster violent behavior toward human or nonhuman beings spring from the same roots and may be prevented or treated in the same or similar ways. Society's goals should be to: (1) prevent the onset of violent behavior with educational and experimental programs that promote nurturing and empathy in children; (2) identify the manifestation of violence at the earliest possible age so that treatment may be initiated; (3) perfect and support intervention programs that successfully reduce acts of violence in an individual and motivate positive behavior patterns."

The National Humane Education Society supports the establishment of programs to educate animal and human service professionals on the shared roots of violence, to promote awareness and acceptance by the public of the need to promote caring attitudes, and to develop a network of multi-disciplinary, community-based protection personnel to combat violence and promote nurturing.

Finally, we also endorse treatment programs that provide empathetic role models, offer a safe outlet for the expression of negative emotions, and build competence and skill in expressing caring, nurturing feelings.

II. *Some Model Efforts*

One agency that is actively responding to this issue is the San Francisco Department of Animal Care and Control. The Department's cooperative relationship with the San Francisco Child Abuse Council has resulted in a number of promising cross-training programs. Animal cruelty investigators are taught to recognize the signs of child abuse, while social workers and police officers learn the symptoms of animal cruelty and neglect.

"If an animal control or state humane officer enters a home and suspects the children are being abused, they report it to the police department," says Ken White, Deputy Director of the San Francisco Department of Animal Care and Control. "And if the police enter a home and feel an animal is being abused, they call us. We're even working to introduce state legislation to put animal care and control investigators on the list of professionals legally required to report suspected child abuse."

By working more closely together, social service and animal welfare agencies can share their findings and intervene more effectively and quickly in breaking children out of this cycle of violence against animals and humans.

Programs that offer children a chance to relate with animals offer one possible solution. A model program run by Green Chimneys in Brewster, N.Y., brings children who are emotionally impaired, learning disabled, or juvenile offenders together with some 150 animals, which these children nurture and care for. The Brewster center where the youngsters stay is also home to pigs, goats, chickens, horses, and other animals.

The goal of Green Chimneys is to build a child's self-esteem and create a nurturing and caring individual. Children in the program experience the therapeutic value of assisting in the animals' daily care; they also learn respect for the animals as they spend more time living among them.

It is primarily through programs such as Green Chimneys and cross-training programs that we will be able to turn wayward children around and prevent the violent abuse of animals and humans. I hold out much promise that this issue can become a thing of the past, *provided* that public education is vigorous and therapeutic programs are available to all the children who need them.

CHAPTER 4

Research, Testing, and Education With Live Animals: A Study In Needless Practices

I. *Is Dissection In Biology Class Really Necessary?*

This question is very much alive in the minds of teachers and students, as well as in our legal system. A controversial court case involving Jenifer Graham, a 15-year old student who objected on moral grounds to dissecting a frog in her biology class, has caused society to take a second look at the practice of experimenting on animals in the classroom.

The case against dissection in biology is multi-faceted. There are moral and religious considerations, as well as the inordinate expense involved in dissection experiments.

Dissection became a widely accepted practice in the 1920s, before low-cost visual aids and films became available to study biology. Today, lab experimentation still involves a good deal of dissection.

When asked to perform dissections on animals, the initial reaction of most students is distaste. In fact, experiments like these, intended to stimulate students' interest in biology, often cause students to turn from pursuing careers in this field because they were revolted by having to cut up an animal when they were in high school.

So what exactly is the point of dissection? Is it to learn physiology or desensitization?

Although many educators feel that dissection is an inducement to students thinking about work in biology or medicine, statistics indicate that only 40 out of 1,000, or 4% of fifth-grade students, will obtain a science degree. For the vast majority of high-school biology students, a detailed knowledge of dissection techniques will have no useful application in their daily lives.

In addition, the expense involved in carrying out these experiments is high. In these days of "belt-tightening" by our school systems, educators would do well to look at the overall cost impact of dissection as compared with various alternatives. An example should help illustrate my point. Suppose a biology program has 72 students working in teams of two. A conservative cost estimate for preserved specimens for this size class is about $1,200 a year. The same $1,200 could purchase audio-visuals, software, or any number of educational alternatives which would serve and enhance the school's science program for years to come—not just for the current year.

A stronger argument against dissection is that the scope and variety of modern alternatives eliminates the need for this antiquated practice. Anatomical replicas, computer software, sophisticated illustrations, interactive videos, and non-intrusive observation of animals are all excellent alternatives to dissection. They eliminate the revulsion commonly experienced by many students, and they allow for unlimited repetition and the ability to start over to correct a mistake.

And what about the animals? With dissection, the waste of life is enormous. Biological supply houses send approximately three million frogs to the dissecting knife annually. Often captured from the wild, the depletion of frogs in exploited areas has sometimes had serious environmental impacts. In Bangladesh, for example, mass exportation is believed to have resulted in overpopulation of crop-damaging and disease-carrying insects which the frogs once controlled. In the late 1960s, the high usage of frogs seriously depleted the native North American species, *Rana pipiens*.

Besides frogs, countless cats, fetal pigs, and other animals are used for classroom dissection. Pounds, slaughter houses, and pet stores all contribute "resources" to this multi-million dollar business. Sometimes, the means of procuring animals is questionable. Live animals slated for biological experiments often suffer from the trauma of confinement, inadequate food and care, crude transport, and inhumane killing methods.

Fortunately, many schools are beginning to call a halt to dissection. Every year, the number of school boards that reject dissection as an educational device is increasing. A survey conducted by *The Science Teacher* determined that 21% of secondary school biology teachers no longer perform dissections. Some find that it doesn't meet their objectives. Others say they can better prepare their students for college with more concept-oriented experiences.

Teachers who still conduct dissection in their classes are also becoming more receptive to students' requests for alternative assignments. Even at many colleges, medical and veterinary curriculums no longer require experiments on animals.

Although there are many logical and scientific reasons for abandoning the practice of dissection, perhaps the most important is reverence for life. At home, parents teach their children to treat their pets with respect and kindness. Our educational system should reinforce that message by forsaking a practice that conflicts with the basic human instinct of compassion for living creatures.

II. *The Needless Suffering of Animals*

The scope of the problem goes far beyond our schools. Live animals are also used as models in biomedical research and toxicity testing. Up to 70 million animals suffer needlessly each year because of inhumane practices such as inducing sicknesses, injuries, or killing—all in the name of testing a product, a virus, new medicines, and a host of other things. If the animals don't die from the effects of the test, they often suffer from neglect, ignorance, indifference, or outright cruelty on the part of lab personnel.

No one wants to see animals suffer, regardless of one's opinion about the ethics of live-animal-related research and other cruel practices. For this reason alone, non-animal alternatives must be accepted in laboratory procedures and testing to reduce pain and other needless suffering. Replacement, reduction, and refinement constitute the three "R's" of the alternatives approach. The goal of humane individuals is the complete replacement of live animals in such practices and the adoption of alternatives.

III. *A Case Study Of Grossly Inhumane Military Animal Experiments*

April 7, 1992, was a milestone in the history of the animal rights movement. On that day, a subcommittee of the U.S. House Committee on Armed Services held hearings on the use of live animals in research by the Department of Defense (DOD).

The subcommittee heard testimony of leading animal rights advocates, including Dr. Martin Stephens of the Humane Society of the United States, about grossly inhumane animal experiments proposed and carried out by DOD researchers. For example:

• tests of the effects of gunfire noise on the Army's K-9 Corps dogs;

• dogs were injected with drugs and then hung in slings and shot to determine the kinds of wounds inflicted;

• turtles fed under inhumane conditions were collected and killed;

• pigs were hung in flack jackets and slings and then subjected to explosives to test the protection given by certain ballistics vests;

• cats placed in canvas bags attached to metal plates were blasted with the noise of rifles and cannons to measure hearing loss;

• monkeys were locked in full-body casts and rotated 90 degrees every 30 minutes for two weeks, and then killed to study the effects of this procedure on their jaw bones;

• monkeys, dogs and rats were exposed to lethal doses of radiation to see how soldiers would fare in a nuclear war;

• goats, dogs, and rabbits were thrown from speeding vehicles to determine injuries that could result from a nuclear blast shock wave; and

• rats, mice, and sheep were subjected to laser rays to determine the rays' potential effects on military personnel.

The House subcommittee in hearings found that 41 military facilities conducted such barbarous research on 300,000 animals in fiscal 1990 at a cost of more than $100 million. DOD officials overseeing such research claimed that it was for the sake of protecting military personnel from disease, injury, and death; however, many veterinarians, animal rights officials, and even medical doctors considered the results of much of this research worthless or inconclusive with regard to human beings.

Members of the subcommittee were so moved by the testimony given on April 7 that they persuaded the committee as a whole to attach a report to the DOD budget authorization bill under consideration for fiscal year 1993. The bill cleared Congress with the report and went to the White House for the President's signature in October 1992.

The House committee report requested that the Secretary of Defense should submit a comprehensive annual report to the House and Senate Armed Services Committees on the use of animals in DOD activities. The DOD was instructed to define:

• initiatives to promote alternative methods that would replace, reduce, and refine the uses of animals in research;

• procedures to avoid duplicative, unnecessary research;

• the chain of command over the animal care and use programs from the individual facility up to the Secretary of Defense; and

• the total cost of animal-based research in comparison to other forms of biological research conducted by the facilities, the military service, and the department as a whole.

Beyond these important recommendations, the DOD bill report directed the Secretary to establish aggressive and targeted programs to replace, reduce, or refine current uses of animals in research.

Appointing an ombudsperson at each animal research facility was also requested to address public concerns about animal care and use programs. In addition, animal rights advocates were to be selected as *bona fide* community members of animal care and use committees at the facilities.

The DOD Inspector General recommended a review of every departmental program, project, or activity concerning the conduct of any type of live-animal research. This official would then issue a report on whether animals used in each program, project, or activity were handled and treated in accordance with the Animal Welfare Act,

DOD regulations, and rules of basic humane treatment in live-animal research.

Finally, the DOD bill report called for the General Accounting Office (GAO) to review and report on every program, project, or activity funded by DOD conducting any type of live-animal research. The GAO was to identify overlap between projects and activities and recommend where funds could be saved.

With this DOD bill, progress was made in the movement for animal rights. Congress had been won over to a humane concern for the treatment of animals in military research, favoring the elimination of grossly inhumane projects.

The National Humane Education Society sides with animal rights advocates who seek to eliminate all gruesome experiments conducted by our armed forces. Of course, we want our military personnel to be spared from injury, disease, and death in warfare, but studies from past conflicts have yielded more valid findings than anything coming from experiments on live animals.

We will continue to express our outrage when such barbarous experiments are proposed for federal funding. There is no doubt that the most effective point at which to halt these experiments is while they are being discussed on Capitol Hill for inclusion in fiscal year budget allocations. Like the authors of the Fiscal Year 1993 DOD bill in the House of Representatives, others in Congress should be alerted to deny funding for senseless inhumane projects.

Finally, the U.S. Department of Agriculture (USDA), which is charged with enforcing the Animal Welfare Act, does not monitor DOD compliance. This regrettable oversight should be corrected by Congress, which can authorize the USDA to conduct and report on such monitoring for compliance.

IV. *Why Defenders Want To Use Live Animals*

Those who defend the use of live animals in biomedical research, testing, and education say the practice has four beneficial applications:

1. To provide fundamental biological knowledge upon which disease prevention and treatment can be based,

2. To provide models for the study of actual diseases of humans and animals,

3. To test potential therapies, diagnostic and surgical procedures, and medical devices, and

4. To study the safety of new drugs or determine potential toxicity of chemicals to which humans and animals will be exposed.

These scientists and researchers insist they need live animals to develop drugs for treatment of cancer, diabetes, Alzheimer's disease, and infectious agents. They claim that many advances in diagnosis, medical treatment, surgical procedures, and pain-killing agents over the last century would not have been possible without animal models in biomedical research.

Because of these advances, they say, Americans can now expect to enjoy more than 70 years of productive life and good health. Experiments on live animals offer the greatest hope for finding the cause, treatment, and prevention of the diseases that inflict pain, disability, and death on millions of people each year. Live-animal studies also assure a more healthful environment and safer consumer products.

Therefore, they claim, continued advances in biomedical research depend on the public's support for using live animals in research. If the public tries to eliminate or severely restrict research on live animals, they will be sacrificing a healthier future for themselves and for generations to come—just to save a few animals.

V. *What Humane People Believe About Alternatives*

Humane people deplore biomedical research, testing, and education using live mice, rats, birds, frogs, hamsters, guinea pigs, rabbits, dogs, cats, primates, and other animals.

Humane individuals and groups believe that medical, biological, psychological and military research, and safety testing can be effectively carried out without using live animals. Tests can be conducted for cosmetics, household products, and other substances equally effectively without using live animals, and biology classes can study anatomy without experimenting with or dissecting animals.

Humane people object to infecting, irradiating, poisoning, burning, cooking, and even shooting animals and housing others in tiny, barren cages—even in the name of science.

Americans enjoy healthier, longer lives because of strides in biomedical research, but none of the progress has directly resulted from testing with live animals. Rather, improvements have stemmed primarily from disease prevention. Americans have better diets, drink and eat less harmful consumer products, and have better access to sanitary water, all contributing to improved health.

In addition, advances have been made in developing more effective, more valid alternatives to the use of live animals in biomedical research. These alternatives include the use of:

1. Cell and tissue culture in test tubes;
2. Deceased and severely diseased persons, who willingly offer their bodies for research in the hope that a cure might be found—if not for them, then at least for future generations;
3. Micro-organisms and creatures with little or no capacity for pain and other suffering;

4. Computer models to answer questions and guide research, testing, and educational classroom dissections; and

5. Fewer repetitive and poorly planned projects.

VI. *The Official Policy of the National Humane Education Society*

Our Society endorses these alternatives, which effectively allow for the complete elimination of live animals in research and other practices. Specifically, we support the following ethical practices:

1. Tissue culture of human muscle can be used instead of mice to determine whether certain substances cause or prevent cancer.

2. In vitro (test-tube) tests with blood cells derived from horseshoe crabs and other primitive creatures are preferable in testing for the presence of fever-causing substances.

3. Research at the National Cancer Institute involves a computer program that models relationships between the human body's immune system and cancer. And medical students in California use computer-assisted manikins to practice medical procedures which previously required live animals.

4. Tissue-culture research has successfully isolated and identified the causes of AIDS—without the use of a single live animal. This humane procedure is also being used to test drugs more rapidly for treatment of the AIDS virus.

As an example of the greater efficiency of alternatives, consider that traditional consumer testing with live animals can take three to four years, cost millions of dollars, and consume thousands of live animals. Even then, tests often have little validity.

By contrast, a battery of non-animal alternatives costs only $25-50,000 and takes only an average of three months. Between 2,000-3,000 tests per year could be made for the same cost. This is in striking contrast to traditional live-animal tests.

Consider the practices of one humane-minded pharmaceutical company. In 1963, this company tested 1,000 substances using 16,000 mice. Twelve years after adopting in vitro techniques, the company tested 22,000 substances in a year, reducing the number of mice sacrificed to 1,600. The ultimate goal is to eliminate the need for sacrificing all mice.

The official policy of the National Humane Education Society is to champion and support research aimed at developing even more alternatives to the use of live animals in biomedical research, testing, and education. If the public continues to avoid harmful consumer products such as alcohol and tobacco and to eat healthier foods low in fat and cholesterol, we should see great strides in human health—greater than any research could produce, whether on live animals or not. Other practices such as daily exercise will lead to further progress in disease prevention and human longevity.

VII. *Conclusion*

Developing and using alternatives to live animals in biomedical research is an encouraging prospect, especially given the relatively small investment of money and effort. Technical advances are already being translated into tangible results, not only in terms of animal welfare, but also in improvements in public health and reduction of costs for treatment. The public's concern for live animal welfare is directly responsible for this progress.

The application of alternatives should ultimately lead to the complete elimination of live animals for laboratory research, product safety testing, and education. What is needed now is more concerted support by researchers, toxicologists, educators, funding agencies, and regulatory agencies for the new alternatives.

Whether this will happen depends in large part on public enthusiasm. As a first step, lay people should familiarize themselves with alternative approaches. This will enable them to recognize as false the wild exaggerations made by people who insist on live-animal research.

Researchers would take alternatives more seriously if more people became informed—and vocal—about humane practices and techniques. Researchers and lay persons share the responsibility and the need to replace animals with "lower" life forms or other tools in laboratory procedures, testing, and education. If this goal is met, our current image of research animals huddled in tiny cages will be replaced with more heartening images—images that don't have to take away the dignity, well-being, and lives of the creatures we were put on earth to protect.

CHAPTER V

The Puppy Mill Scandal

"How Much is That Doggie in the Window?" has become one of the classic songs of Christmas. It's also a question many people find themselves asking at that time of year, even though reason tells them they shouldn't give it a second thought.

Giving a pet to a child for Christmas can be an irresistible proposition, even when it should be resisted. Every year, as many as 500,000 fathers and mothers buy puppies from pet stores because they can't say "no" to the "doggie in the window."

There is no doubt that puppies are appealing— kittens, too. It takes strong resolution to carefully assess the decision to acquire a pet and to weigh carefully the many responsibilities that come with a pet as it scampers across your threshold.

Parents need to ask themselves some difficult questions like: "Is my child old enough to care for a puppy?" "Will my home offer long-term care of the kitten?" "Is there a good chance my child will quickly tire of the pet?" "Will the new pet be abandoned with the tree and tinsel and wind up in a pound to be 'put to sleep' because we can't take care of it?"

It is sobering to think of what can happen to that puppy or kitten in the pet store window when you bring it home— and then a day comes when no one wants to care for it.

It is even more sobering to think of what happens to animals in commercial kennels and pet stores, where owners are primarily concerned with the profits they can generate from mass births.

All too often "puppy mills" are little concerned for the well-being of the precious lives they helped to create. Only contempt can explain the gross conditions in which many owners breed and keep these helpless little animals.

I. *The Scope of the Problem*

A few years ago, Robert Baker, an inspector of the Humane Society of the United States, conducted a survey of puppy mills in America. He found that more than half of them failed miserably to meet approved standards for housing, feeding, and sanitation.

"Many of the violations were appalling," says Baker. "Fecal material piled two feet high in dog runs, puppies' feet trapped in wire mesh cage floors, the use of dog carcasses as feed for dogs, and extreme overcrowding."

Despite the public outcry and reforms the Baker Report precipitated, conditions in many puppy mills remain atrocious. Last year, Mr. Baker made a random, spot inspection of 25 puppy mills and found them to be as bad as they were before. "In fact, one place was even worse than any place I'd ever seen," he says.

People for the Ethical Treatment of Animals (PETA) describes the ills of puppy mills as follows: "Puppy mill kennels usually consist of small wood and wire-mesh cages, or even empty crates or trailer cabs, all kept outdoors, where female dogs are bred continuously, with no rest between heat cycles. The mothers and their children often suffer from malnutrition, exposure, and lack of adequate veterinary care. Continuous breeding takes its toll on the females, and they are killed when their bodies give out and they no longer can produce enough litters."

All groups concerned with animal welfare—even some state and federal officials—agree that many of the puppies and the female adults used in breeding are subjected to inhumane conditions, not only in kennels, but also in shipment to pet stores and in the stores themselves.

The problem of puppy mills became particularly distressing after World War II, when the demand for puppies rose dramatically. Breeding conditions became so outrageous that Congress, in 1966, passed the Animal Welfare Act. The goal of the Act was to alleviate the inhumane conditions under which puppies are bred in kennels and transported to stores.

The Animal Welfare Act is regulated by the Animal and Plant Health Inspection Service (APHIS) of the U.S. Department of Agriculture (USDA). The law requires breeders to be licensed and authorizes APHIS to conduct inspections regularly and to follow up on complaints of inhumane conditions in puppy mills.

Violators are given 30 days to correct improper practices. When a reinspection is made, if the recommendations have not been carried out, legal action is brought against the breeder. Fines and penalties, including loss of license, are severe enough, say APHIS officials, to discourage puppy mills from persisting in inhumane practices.

In 1987, USDA inspectors visited 6,732 licensed facilities at an average rate of 1.6 times per site to enforce compliance. Of these, 145 violations were forwarded to the USDA General Counsel for action. Forty-four cases resulted in the imposition of license suspensions or revocations, cease-and-desist orders, civil penalties, or a combination of these sanctions. In addition, USDA issued warnings to another 180 less serious violators.

However, many humane groups contend that the USDA severely underestimates the number of breeding kennels that are guilty of inhumane conditions. They also charge that USDA inspectors often deliberately overlook improprieties. Whereas Robert Baker found a 50% rate of serious non-compliance among the 300 puppy mills he investigated in 1981, USDA inspectors who visited the 158 kennels Baker had judged to be bad cited only 35 for having one or more violations. Of 7,000 facilities inspected by USDA in 1987, fewer than 2% had formal action brought against them for repeated, critical, or flagrant violations.

Whatever the true incidence of inhumane conditions, one trend appears significant: small "mom-and-pop" puppy mills are worse than large-scale concerns. The reason? Larger for-profit breeders are more readily prosecuted and fined, but they also have the resources to correct unacceptable conditions; small dealers are harder to regulate. Although they, too, can breed large numbers of pets, they have limited funds to make the necessary corrections. If called to account for inhumane conditions, smaller operators can often play upon the sympathy and leniency of local judges who are prone to let them off, citing extenuating circumstances.

The USDA admits that it needs the states' help to cope with the problem of inspections. "APHIS has only so much staff and cannot be at all puppy mills, so we are limited in the number we can inspect each year," says Dr. Richard Crawford, senior APHIS veterinarian. "If the states pitch in, combining their inspections with ours would go further to assure humane breeding practices."

Dr. Crawford sees a definite role to be played by humane groups and humane individuals in enforcement activity. Federal and state inspections will be more effective, he says, if they are directed toward offenders who have already had complaints leveled against them by the public. An informed citizenry willing to report on offending breeders and pet stores will go a long way toward eliminating the needless suffering that so many animals now endure.

In addition, humane groups and pet industry associations can help eliminate inhumane conditions by educating and motivating breeders to follow proper operating procedures. "An informed pet industry living up to acceptable standards is the best approach to assuring humane conditions in breeding kennels," says Dr. Crawford.

The executive director of the Pet Industry Joint Advisory Council (PIJAC), Marshall Meyers, agrees. "While it is not realistic to think we can do away with regulations, I can foresee the time when, by education, inhumane practices will be eliminated," Mr. Meyers says.

There is a glaring gap, however, in enforcement and education which everyone agrees should be drawn around the bad actors in the industry: namely, that pet stores are not subject to APHIS regulation and inspection.

Writing in the humane magazine, *The Animal Agenda*, author Jack Rosenberg says, "pet shop owners can literally get away with murder...because the pet industry is loosely regulated. The ordinances and laws for pet shops are supposed to induce compliance. But the frequency of inspections, the degree of law enforcement, even the definition of a pet shop vary greatly from county to county, and from state to state."

Mr. Rosenberg cites the example of a Maryland man who owned two pet stores, each in a different county. He closed one store because county inspectors threatened to prosecute him for violations of county ordinances, whereas in the other county he encountered no objections. He had managed both stores identically.

Pet abuse during transportation also needs close attention. The manner in which cats and dogs are shipped from breeding kennels to retail outlets is frequently a scandal. "Shipment from the puppy mills by brokers who ship to pet shops can cover hundreds of miles by pick-up trucks, tractor trailers, and/or planes, often without adequate food, water, ventilation, or shelter," reports PETA. Transportation is supposed to be subject to APHIS inspection, but it appears from the PETA report that a more vigorous application of the regulations is needed.

Retired Congressman Manuel Lujan is among those who think a study should be made of the effectiveness of current laws. He proposed a joint resolution intended to find ways of tightening regulations so that pets will be protected all along the chain of pet breeding, transportation, and retail sale.

II. *The Official Position of the National Humane Education Society*

The National Humane Education Society believes the breeding, transportation, and sale of pets must be conducted under the most humane conditions possible, in order to prevent needless suffering. This means requiring pet wholesalers, shipping companies, and pet shop retailers to meet and maintain standards that will guarantee the humane well-being of the animals in their care.

The Society agrees with those who hold that scandalous, inhumane conditions in the pet industry continue to be widespread. We believe that education will help to redress these wrongs, but we are convinced that strict enforcement of federal and local regulations is also essential. More, not fewer, inspections are called for, particularly in the areas of transportation and retail sale of pets. It is unrealistic to assume that the pet industry can or will regulate itself without outside pressures.

The Society holds that humane individuals and groups have a major role to play in preventing animal abuse. Responsibilities include:

• Reporting operators found to abuse the pets in their care;

• Helping to establish humane standards for the pet industry; and

• Encouraging people who want pets to adopt them from shelters, rather than from pet stores or breeding kennels.

We believe that it is foolish and wasteful of many good lives to breed hundreds of thousands of pets each year while the nation's shelters are overcrowded with unwanted and unclaimed pets destined for euthanasia.

III. *What You Can Do To Help*

If friends tell you they are looking to buy a pet, encourage them to look at their local animal shelter first. If they insist on a purebred, advise them to buy from an area breeder, and to visit his facilities to assure themselves that their future pet was raised in humane surroundings. Remember, too, that animal shelters and humane societies often take in many lovely pure-bred animals.

If you see what appears to be a sick or abused animal in a pet shop, call your local health department immediately. Report the conditions you observed and ask them to investigate the situation for themselves. Notify your local humane society of your concern and the action you have taken.

Help your local humane society work for stricter enforcement of humane regulations and for the passage of tougher local ordinances and state laws governing the sale of animals in pet stores.

Contact your senators and your congressional representative and urge them to support a study of the Animal Welfare Act to make sure dogs and puppies are protected from inhumane treatment in breeding, transportation, and retail pet stores.

Finally, support groups such as the National Humane Education Society, which spreads the word through educational campaigns and provides hands-on care of abandoned cats and dogs at Peace Plantation.

"Buy me that doggie in the window?"

If you think it will get the care it deserves, say "yes"—but say "yes" to the one in the window of Peace Plantation (or any other animal shelter), where respect for life is the standard, and the care given to animals is as bright and shining as the Christmas star.

CHAPTER VI

Hunting—
What Are We After?

Hunting is the seeking, pursuit, and killing of wild animals. To prehistoric man, hunting was a necessity, as the quarry provided food from the meat and clothing from the skins.

Records of the past also show the ingenuity and inventiveness of the hunters, and the materials and technology available to them. Weapons at first ranged from sticks, stones, and specially shaped clubs to sharp, pointed spears. Next, the bow and arrow became the weapon of choice, making the hunt somewhat more successful. But stealth and relentless pursuit played the major role in the kill. In modern times, guns have supplanted most other methods; guns have dramatically changed the nature of hunting.

Today, people no longer need to hunt wild animals for food. Farmers grow fruit, vegetables, and grains and raise livestock and poultry for food. A select number of individuals, however, still hunt sport. Wildlife managers also invite hunters to help control populations of animals.

Controversy today surrounds the concern of whether hunting should continue for any purpose, because the practice undeniably causes much needless suffering.

I. *Arguments For and Against Hunting*

A. *"Managed Hunting"*

Lonnie Williamson, a biologist and an official of the Wildlife Management Institute, advocates hunting as "a recreational and management tool commonly permitted in certain areas and at certain times to maintain predetermined numbers of wildlife populations. Hunting helps to minimize agricultural, forested, and horticultural damages while providing recreational opportunities, food, and other benefits. In some communities, farms, grazing lands, and woodlots, hunting is a source of income through expenditures of hunters."

With well-designed regulations and proper management, hunting can eliminate only those animals that could be replaced through natural reproduction; in this sense, hunting is similar to harvesting agricultural crops. Products are taken from the environment for the benefit of humans, but the sources can rejuvenate the animal population through reproduction.

Of course, some animals withstand hunting better than others. Wildlife managers therefore should assess the numbers that can safely be killed without endangering the overall population. Hunters should be allowed to kill only if there is a surplus that may be harvested without impairing the basic breeding stock.

Williamson states, "Populations of animals that live in isolated environments or have very specific habitat requirements can be overhunted if the harvest is not regulated closely. Managed hunting, however, prevents taking excess numbers."

Williamson argues that hunting does not decimate wildlife populations, "because the killing is regulated so that only excess numbers may be taken."

Williamson would also take exception to people who think wild animals should not be hunted in the name of recreation: "Whoever does the hunting and for whatever reason, the practice serves as a wildlife management tool."

Perhaps the main reason for his belief in the need for hunting is economic: hunters pay taxes on guns and ammunition. These taxes are used by states for conservation measures designed to enhance the population of wild creatures. Money is also collected from permits paid for by hunters, and these millions of dollars are spent in improving habitats, so creatures can thrive. So, not only hunters benefit. Bird watchers and others interested in wild animal behavior can take advantage of the money poured back into conservation and preservation of the creatures' environments.

B. An Unnecessary Practice

Dr. John W. Grandy, an official with the Humane Society of the United States, has for many years been studying hunting and its effects on wildlife. In a speech he made at a conference entitled "Animals and Humans," Grandy noted that "hunting is supposed to be a recreational pastime but is little more than shooting at animated targets. People don't hunt for food; they predominantly derive pleasure from killing animals."

Even if all animals killed by hunters were available for eating, the practice would still be wholly unnecessary. Americans don't need to eat the flesh of hunted animals, because they can satisfy their demand for meat through domesticated cattle, sheep, swine, and poultry, raised precisely for their food.

The basic question, according to Grandy, is whether state and federal governments will continue to permit the killing of wildlife as an acceptable form of recreation. Hunters inflict much needless cruelty—pain, trauma, wounding, and premature death—to living, feeling creatures. It's difficult to justify such suffering and killing in the name of fun.

Grandy also takes on the federal and state wildlife managers and hunters who say hunting is needed to control wildlife populations. According to this view, animals would overpopulate their habitats and die of starvation if allowed to reproduce indefinitely and unhindered.

Grandy counters this belief by stating, "most of our country provides sufficient forage for animals. Nature has provided natural controls over population growth. As animals increase in numbers, reproduction falls off. Some die of natural causes such as disease and starvation, but these are usually the aged and sick. Healthy young creatures will, without hunting, survive and provide vigor to the future generations. Hunters disregard this, as they go after the healthiest stock to gain trophies and to brag about their success at hunting."

And not only is hunting permitted on many acres of publicly and privately owned lands, federal managers also allow hunting on many national wildlife refuges. These lands and waters were set aside to provide havens for animals so they could thrive. Now these havens have become hell-holes for many creatures.

"How can we refer to these lands and waters as animal refuges when the creatures within them are not safe because of hunting?" asks Grandy. "Hunting is not a scientific management tool. If wildlife must be managed, managers should rely upon scientific methodology, which would greatly reduce needless suffering and provide ample opportunities for the young and vigorous stock to pass on their superior traits to ensuing populations."

Hunting with guns is not a true sport. Animals are no match for rifles and shotguns. Even bows and arrows are inhumane—particularly when they don't instantly kill, but result in senseless, lingering suffering. Viewing wildlife with cameras and binoculars is a true sport and is the only form of "shooting" that should be tolerated on the wildlife refuges and other habitats where wild creatures thrive.

II. *The Official Policy of the National Humane Education Society*

Our Society has strong reservations about hunting. This practice hardly qualifies as an acceptable form of sport, because animals are no match for high-powered rifles and scope shotguns. Sport is an activity in which participants match up equally with adversaries and provide a true challenge to one another, and hunting does not fall under this rubric.

Hunting can hardly be a management tool to enhance wildlife either. For one, hunting is not a scientific means. The success or failure of hunters cannot be predicted; nor can hunters anticipate precisely which kinds of animals they will shoot.

Indeed, hunters frequently bag the wrong types of animals for "management" purposes. Instead of taking old and sick creatures, which might be considered a humane measure, hunters most often target the healthiest and strongest specimens. Of course, by maiming and killing the best, hunters prevent the quarry from passing on superior traits through propagation to offspring.

The argument that hunting is necessary to control population and to prevent animals from overfeeding the environment is also dubious. Much of our country still has ample forage to support populations of wild creatures. As populations grow, the birth rate of the animals falls naturally; nature left to her own devices will exert controls over population growth.

Our Society also asks, "How can amateur hunters be effective in controlling animal populations humanely?" Inexperienced hunters often wound animals, which then suffer slow, painful deaths.

The major argument for hunting cited by some biologists is economic: since the taxes and permit fees hunters pay are spent on improving habitats, hunters have the right to kill wild creatures.

The Society views such an argument as specious because animals belong to all people, not just to the small fraction of those who hunt. If money is needed for wildlife enhancement, it can come from general government revenues drawn from the taxes paid by all citizens. Hunters have no inherent right or special privilege to kill animals just because they pay special excise taxes.

Leaders in the animal rights and welfare movement are working to inform the public about hunting—and its many abuses. Through educational programs revealing the truth about hunting, we intend to convey the message that hunting is not good sport and is a very poor management tool.

The policy of the National Humane Education Society therefore is:

1. We are opposed to hunting for sport, trophy, or for any other purpose. Such killing sets a terrible impression on our young people, who watch their elders kill creatures without the slightest remorse. No civilized society should condone such senseless, brutal killing of wild creatures.

2. Calling certain wild animals "game" is objectionable. This term belittles the intrinsic value of wild animals as living, sensitive creatures strongly imbued with the desire to live and reproduce. Like humans, wild creatures have the right to life—and this right of theirs ought to be respected.

3. Animals have rights that deserve to be respected. They thrive and reproduce and should not be denied the right to live out their lives fully and purposely.

4. The only wildlife sports which deserve to be encouraged are spectator sports using cameras and binoculars. Observing animals is humane and educational; participants can learn a great deal about the appearance and behavior of creatures in the wild, without having to harm them.

CHAPTER VII

Commercial Trapping:
An Idea Whose Time Has Gone

Commercial trapping is the use of snares to catch, hold, and kill animals for their pelts. A remnant of the mass killing of wild animals that took place from the 1600s through the 1800s, such trapping continues today because high values are placed on animal furs. Whereas market hunting for meat, feathers, and pelts has been outlawed throughout our country, commercial trapping is allowed and encouraged by state and federal agencies concerned with wild animals.

In North America, the Indians were the first to trap, using primitive snares and covered pits dug in the ground to catch animals for their food and hides. Next, European trappers arrived with more effective snares in the 17th century in search of animals for pelts.

Because of the demand for meat, feathers, and hides, commercial hunting and trapping decimated populations of wild creatures in the West in the 19th century. Along with the nearly total extinction of buffaloes, elk, antelopes, and other so-called game animals that market gunners went west for, trappers seriously depleted populations of beavers, bobcats, lynx, mink, skunks, raccoons, fishers, martens, wolverines, wolves, and bears.

By the end of the 19th century, leaders in business and government, including Theodore Roosevelt, who were outraged by the abusive practices and unsportsmanlike behavior of market hunters and trappers, formed clubs that actively lobbied for strong hunting and trapping regulations and effective enforcement.

With the onset of the conservation movement in the United States, a groundswell of public opinion induced the states and the federal government to assume regulatory power over wildlife harvests. As a result, today, state wildlife agencies control trapping and hunting by limiting harvests to certain seasons and by setting quotas on the kinds and numbers of wild creatures that can be taken.

I. The Trap To End All Traps

Driving the fur trade throughout the 19th and 20th centuries was the development of new, more efficient traps and trapping techniques—the most notable being the tooth-jaw leghold trap and its descendant, the steel-jaw leghold trap. Several other traps are also used by trappers, but they are not nearly as popular or effective as the steel-jaw leghold trap.

Most trappers in North America today favor the steel-jaw leghold trap, and it is considered the preeminent factor in the great wealth of designers and marketers of fur garments. Indeed, economists estimate that the fur garment industry is worth several hundred million dollars. While some of this value results from ranchers raising mink and foxes, the main sources of fur income come from trapped wild creatures.

The steel-jaw leghold trap is a spring-powered device with a weight-sensitive pan and two fixed metal jaws. When a paw or beak comes in contact with the pan, the jaws snap shut on the body part with a force equal to a car door slamming shut on a human hand.

Estimates of the number of animals taken solely for pelts run as high as 15 million per year. These include foxes, coyotes, badgers, mink, skunks, rabbits, prairie dogs, otters, and squirrels. Millions of other creatures are captured unintentionally, since the traps will snare any creature touching the triggering pan. Even endangered bald-headed eagles have been snared and left to die in the traps, along with other eagles, hawks, owls, and vultures.

II. *Commercial Trapping And The Steel-Jaw Leghold Trap: Pro & Con*

A. *Arguments For*

According to Greg Linscombe, a Louisiana wildlife biologist, trapping is necessary in some areas of the country either to control wild animal populations or to preserve habitat. "In either case," Linscombe says, "unless animal populations are harvested, large numbers will certainly die from disease, starvation or by being killed by other animals."

Linscombe adds, "Preservation of our environment and satisfying the needs of society dictate the use of professional wildlife management techniques. A crisis in the Louisiana wetlands exists, in part, because of a serious overpopulation of nutria and muskrats, which are destroying the wetlands vegetation. If we could not trap in these wetlands, a large portion of coastal Louisiana would be adversely affected. This would mean a staggering loss to our seafood industry and a loss of habitat essential to migratory water fowl and to hundreds of other species of birds and mammals dependent on these wetlands."

In Louisiana, the Department of Wildlife and Fisheries controls trapping by prescribing the seasons when animals can be trapped and the kinds of species that can be legally taken.

Linscombe argues that "Trappers catch excess animals in the populations. In doing so, they remove animals that would otherwise be lost to natural mortality, such as disease, fighting, and starvation. By slowing population growth, the trapping often helps keep muskrats and other animals from growing in numbers so much that they exceed the carrying capacity of the habitat. Trappers therefore help animal numbers within the carrying capacity of the habitat, and thus insure the survival of the habitat and the animal populations it supports.''

Linscombe acknowledges that questions have arisen concerning the physical injury of animals caught in steel-jaw leghold traps. ''But whatever the injury may be,'' he says, ''it is no doubt much more humane than a slow agonizing death caused by disease or starvation.''

Indeed, the National Trappers Association supplies the following reasons in support of the continued use of the steel-jaw leghold trap:

• Domestic animals are seldom harmed by such traps.

• Because of recent improvements in the traps, injuries and suffering have been reduced in trapped animals.

• Few non-furbearing creatures are caught in these traps, which are set specifically for furbearing animals.

• The United States has rightfully resisted banning such traps (unlike more than 50 countries where these traps have been banned).

• Trappers help control populations of wild creatures by snaring those that are more populous much more often than those from sparse populations.

• Traps are checked regularly every day to relieve any suffering endured by trapped creatures.

• Leghold traps are not inhumane and can be used for quick kills of water-oriented creatures, which submerge and are quickly drowned when trapped.

• Cage traps for snaring and holding live creatures are not used extensively by trappers because they are too costly, too visible, too easy to steal, and difficult to transport.

B. *Arguments Against*

Susan Hagood of the Defenders of Wildlife, a group that has been tracking trapping practices for a number of decades, says the arguments of the National Trappers Association are more fiction than fact. In response to the trappers' arguments, Hagood points out:

• There are numerous cases of pets being snared and injured in such traps. Dick Randall, a former Fish and Wildlife Service trapper has said, "my trapping records show that for each target animal I trapped, about two unwanted individuals were caught."

• Scientific research has demonstrated that animals are as sensitive to pain as humans—perhaps even more so.

• The reason our country has thus far not adopted a federal statute banning the steel-jaw leghold trap is not because the public favors this trap; it is because trapping groups have considerable influence in Congress.

• Trappers target the more lucrative animals with no concern for population control. The trappers are interested in making as much money as possible through the sale of pelts.

• We have only the word of the American Trappers Association that traps are checked regularly. We lack definitive field studies on the frequency of trap visitation by trappers.

• Creatures living in and near water, such as muskrats, sometimes sink and drown quickly after being snared in a leghold trap. But target animals such as otters and beavers rarely sink and drown without a lengthy, painful struggle.

• Cage or box traps are available for anyone to use. They may be cumbersome, they may be expensive, but they catch and hold animals humanely. Such traps are widely used in urban areas by humane groups and animal control agents to pick up stray pets.

Four states—Massachusetts, Rhode Island, New Jersey, and Florida—already ban much of the trapping done with the steel-jaw traps. These bans are the direct result of public outcry against such inhumane devices.

Michael O'Sullivan, an official with the World Society for the Protection of Animals who has also studied commercial trapping for many years, soundly rejects the argument that since animals die, there is no reason why they should not be harvested by commercial trappers.

Mr. O'Sullivan agrees that trapped animals, especially those caught in steel-jaw leghold traps, suffer a great deal before they die. Furthermore, trappers catch young, healthy wild animals much more often than they do the sick and aged. Since traps snare as many "non-targeted" animals as they do fur creatures, the argument that trapping keeps animal populations in check is false. Traps are not selective: eagles, hawks, and other wild creatures are often snared and then routinely discarded by trappers.

O'Sullivan believes trappers are now reducing existing populations of lynx, bobcats, and wolverines to near extinction. In previous years, beavers, sea otters, and other species were greatly reduced in numbers due to indiscriminate trapping. In these instances, it was only when wildlife biologists pushed for a halt to trapping and then transplanted the remaining numbers to more hospitable habitats that species were spared total extinction.

O'Sullivan believes state wildlife agencies do a very poor job of determining precisely what limits should be set for trapping. Only by extensive and time-consuming inspections would it be possible to determine the number and kinds of animals surviving—and few, if any, wildlife agencies are prepared to carry out such inventories.

The argument that trapping curtails the spread of diseases such as rabies in animal populations is also false, according to O'Sullivan. Again, because traps don't discriminate, trappers more frequently catch young, healthy animals. As O'Sullivan declares, "We cannot set traps so that only the sick and aged are caught."

And what does Mr. O'Sullivan think about the traps themselves? About 90% of animals that provide pelts are snared by steel-jaw leghold traps, which subject the victims to needless intense suffering. "Indeed, some animals even chew off the paw or leg caught in the trap to halt the intense suffering and to escape."

He adds, "I further believe that the so-called soft catch leghold traps are not more humane. The thin padding of the steel jaws in the traps often does not eliminate the pain. In addition, such traps cost much more, and after one or more catches, the padding is rubbed or chewed off so that trappers are forced to return to the steel-jaw traps."

Commercial trappers today are mostly part-time amateurs who should not be relied upon as sound wildlife managers. O'Sullivan feels "biologists who say trapping is a good management tool for regulating animal populations are mistaken. They cannot extrapolate accurately from past catches what present and future populations will be."

It is ironic that more than 100 national wildlife refuges throughout the United States permit trapping. "Isn't this the precise opposite from why refuges were established in the first place?" asks O'Sullivan. "They were established as havens for all creatures. Trapping them flies in the face of the purpose. The refuges are no longer havens for many creatures caught in traps."

O'Sullivan urges that if people would refrain from buying fur garments, trapping would come to an end for lack of economic incentive. We now have many materials that more effectively guard against the cold than fur.

III. *The Official Policy Of The National Humane Education Society*

The National Humane Education Society believes there is no scientific or ethical justification for commercial trapping. The official position of our Society is as follows:

1. Commercial trapping causes much needless suffering of fur creatures, as well as many other wild and domestic animals caught in traps. Animals are commonly left in traps for two to three days or more, and they are then killed by clubbing or by being stood upon to induce strangulation or suffocation.

2. Most trapping is done with steel-jaw leghold traps, which are cruel, inhumane, and banned in more than 64 countries. These traps inflict a great deal of senseless, useless suffering. Even for legitimate purposes—such as preventing predators from killing livestock—more humane traps are available for snaring and holding wild animals with a minimum of suffering.

3. Commercial trapping is motivated not for the sake of wildlife management, but by the economic incentive in selling pelts. Killing wild animals for profit is ethically wrong.

4. As a wildlife management tool, commercial trapping is not scientifically valid. Traps do not discriminate, since anything that triggers them will be caught. For example, during one U.S. Government attempt to eliminate coyotes, 1,205 animals were trapped, but only 138 of these were coyotes. The remaining 1,067 included bobcats, golden eagles, and 24 other species. Sixty-three of these were domestic animals, including many sheep, which the coyote control program was designed to protect!

5. Nature does a better job of controlling populations of wildlife creatures than does commercial trapping.

6. Commercial trapping of fur creatures for their pelts cannot be justified ethically. Garments made from

synthetic materials offer better protection, at a cheaper cost, and aesthetically just as pleasing.

7. Wearing fur garments is ethically wrong, because furbearing creatures are subjected to much suffering by trappers.

8. Commercial trapping is a holdover from the days of unrestricted market hunting and trapping. Since the first has been banned, it's time to eliminate commercial trapping as well.

IV. *What You Can Do To Show Your Opposition*

The best way to combat this inhumane practice is to stop buying any fur clothing—coats, hats, or other garb. With no market for pelts, the trapping practice would disappear overnight.

In addition, you can apply pressure on lawmakers at the local, state, and national levels. Because trappers already have tremendous influence on state and federal lawmakers, it may be best to start at the county level. Let your elected and appointed officials know how you feel about steel-jaw leghold traps, by calling them and telling them you believe these traps should be banned.

The fight to win a ban will be difficult, but we urge you to persevere—your pressure will pay off in the long run. Remember, we have already won bans in Massachusetts, New Jersey, Rhode Island, and Florida!

And don't forget to write and call the editors of your local newspapers. Tell them you oppose the use of such traps, and encourage them to write editorials favoring a ban. Since their statements get wide play, they have the greatest potential to influence many people.

CHAPTER VIII

Fur Farms: A Bad Alternative

Suppose you, or someone you know, were considering the purchase of a fur garment. A friend of yours tells you that you should buy a fur that came from a fur farm, because it is more "humane" to buy a "raised" fur than a "trapped" one.

Well, in case you're weighing this option, here are a few gruesome facts about fur farming you should know:

• More than 40 million animals are raised under intensive, degrading conditions each year for the fur trade. The main species bred for their fur are mink and fox.

• There are more than 11,000 fur factory farms in Scandinavia, the principal producing region.

• Fur farms consume vast quantities of foodstuffs (including half the Finnish herring catch), since more than one ton of valuable, protein-rich food goes into the production of every full-length coat.

• Selective breeding for consistent color has induced a number of disorders in farmed mink. Stress behaviors such as tail sucking, ear chewing, and fur clipping are extremely common.

• The most popular methods for killing mink are barbiturate injection, inhalation of carbon monoxide (from car exhaust), and neck dislocation.

I. *Fur Farms*

More and more pelts produced for the fur garment industry come from animals raised on fur farms. While the fur industry contends these farms are a humane alternative to trapping animals in the wild, they are most emphatically not.

Representatives of the fur industry emphasize that most pelts from mink and silver fox come from fur farms, thereby diverting attention away from the even less popular steel-trap method of capturing animals. For this reason, few people are aware of the inherent cruelty in fur farming. The fur industry plays on this ignorance, hoping the public will accept fur farms as a humane alternative to trapping.

Toward this goal, the Fur Farm Animal Welfare Coalition has developed a pamphlet for distribution to the public, called "Fur Farming in North America," documenting the "good animal husbandry" practices of fur farms, such as proper nutrition, regular veterinary care, and humane housing and slaughter methods. The pamphlet notes that over three-quarters of the pelts produced in North America come from fur farms; 5.8 million mink and fox pelts, valued at $230 million, were produced by fur farmers in 1986 alone. These numbers are unacceptable to animal rights activists, primarily because the conditions the animals on fur farms endure are inhumane. Animals are restricted to tiny cages and cared for only until their fur is fully developed. Then they are killed by methods designed solely to protect the pelts: breaking their necks, gassing, or electrocution, all of which cause intense suffering before death.

In the United States, while there is some state regulation of fur farms, the industry is self-regulated by and large. The federal government has no statutes governing the living conditions and slaughtering practices of animals raised for furs. The industry has formulated voluntary standards that are not enforceable by law. There is little or no inspection of farm practices, so it is anyone's guess if a given farm provides humane conditions and complies with voluntary practices.

In the absence of federal regulation, animal rights activists have launched a crusade against apparel made from animal pelts. They are encouraged in their efforts by a growing grassroots boycott of fur coats and other garments. Evidence of the move away from fur can be seen from the fall fashion collections of world-class designers such as Bill Blass and Carolina Herrera, who have opted for fabric prints and who shun fur. Popular actresses such as Candice Bergen and Bea Arthur not only refuse to wear furs, they also speak out against the fur industry. For the rest of us, disapproving glances from strangers and negative comments from friends have discouraged many from buying and wearing fur garments.

II. *Yesterday and Today*

In the 19th century, furs became an issue of aesthetics and status, and people began breeding animals in captivity to produce pelts with certain characteristics. By the 1930s, breeders had found the optimum conditions and nutrition needed to raise animals with these select characteristics. This heralded the rise of fur farms, created so that the most sought-after animals (the "silver blue" mink, for example) could be bred on a large scale.

Today, nearly one thousand mink farms produce approximately four million pelts each year. Hundreds more grow chinchilla and nutria pelts. At all of these farms, animals are killed when their coats are at the peak of winter beauty and luxuriance.

Despite the pious claims of the fur industry, animals raised for their pelts suffer cruelly and needlessly. Humane groups are spreading the word throughout the country that clothes can and should be made of synthetic materials rather than fur.

III. *Activists Unite To Fight The Fur Industry*

In 1986, animal rights activists convened in Luxembourg to pronounce formal opposition to the fur industry and to declare war on fur-farming practices in Europe and North America. At no previous time were the various animal rights groups so united, and this union is still in effect today.

The coalition's strategy to end the farming and trapping of animals for fur is a complete boycott of all animal furs and their by-products. The success of this strategy became evident a year later, when the steady growth of the fur industry began to wane as fewer people purchased furs in Western Europe and North America.

Demonstrations, sit-ins, and public service announcements in the print and electronic media are also having a potent effect. More people are now willing to challenge the notion that furs bestow glamour, prestige, and status. Sensitive people concur with animal rights advocates that synthetic garments can gratify human needs at much less cost and without the need for animals to suffer.

Indeed, in the past 10 years, both the amount of trapping and the number of fur farms have declined due to a variety of economic factors. Public awareness of the work of animal rights advocates has helped make fur trapping and farming less lucrative.

A 1992 survey commissioned by the Fur Information Council found that only one American woman in five owns a fur coat. This figure supports their position that the business doesn't need or want to attract a majority to sustain their industry. However, a minority customer base still translates into millions of animals killed annually for their pelts.

With this customer base, the fur industry can also afford to ignore substantial public discomfort with killing animals for fur. In December of 1993, for example, a nationwide Los Angeles Times poll of 1,612 adults found that half opposed the wearing of fur (another 15% were undecided). Nevertheless, an ample 35 percent of the population remained receptive to fur. In addition, the great majority of both fur coat owners and non-owners say they have not been influenced in their purchasing decisions by anti-fur campaigns.

IV. *The Official Policy Of The National Humane Education Society*

The Society stands behind the following principles concerning fur garments fashioned from animal pelts—whether these come from fur farms, trapping, or any other source:

1. Since it is no longer necessary for persons to buy fur garments as protection against the cold, buyers should instead purchase synthetic substitutes. These are readily available, less costly, just as attractive, and every bit as effective in maintaining comfort in winter temperatures.

2. Since some people are uninformed about the cruelties in fur farming, the Society and other humane groups will continue to disseminate true information about fur farms—that they institutionalize the terrible suffering of the vast numbers of animals they exploit. It is therefore fitting that we boycott the end products coming from these farms.

3. Some fur-industry supporters say that, since people kill animals for food, the same principle should apply to fur farming. The National Humane Education Society does not advocate the slaughter of animals for food, and hence does not condone the slaughter of animals for fur. Even if a distinction were made, there is a vast difference between killing animals for food and slaughtering them for vanity.

4. Some people still argue that fur coats are glamorous clothing; they say there is nothing wrong with admiring and buying fur garments made from animal pelts. The Society rejects this idea, since it is built upon the cruel suffering and needless deaths of millions of living creatures.

5. Despite the documented and suspected cruelty, fur farming is left largely unregulated by federal and state governments. The Society will continue to push for tighter regulation of fur farming—if not outlawing it, at least curtailing its most inhumane practices.

Fur farming is another abuse of animal life which every humane man, woman, and child should oppose by refusing to wear fur garments and by boycotting those who make and sell them.

CHAPTER IX

Minimizing Factory Farming

Advances in civilization have not always been for the best. Some of these—like improved transportation, automation, and communications—are undeniable improvements. We can now travel more conveniently, work better, and learn about the world faster and easier than ever before.

But there are certain other "advances" that are more ambiguous. Take food, for example. Is it really an improvement to have foods available year-round on the shelves of our supermarkets—when they are often filled with deadly chemicals?

Are we doing ourselves a favor by having chicken and beef on our tables four or five times a week, when the conditions chicken and cattle are raised under are truly inhumane, not to mention that these conditions raise serious questions about the quality of the meats and poultry we consume?

Let's take a closer look at a peculiarly "modern" phenomenon called "factory farming."

I. *What Is Factory Farming?*

In the last 50 years, the United States and other countries have revolutionized poultry and livestock production for food. As animal scientist Joy A. Mench has said, "remarkable increases in the efficiency of poultry and livestock production have occurred in many industrialized nations. Many factors have contributed [including] artificial selection, advances in the detection, treatment, and prevention of disease, mechanization of farm labor . . . and the development of nutritionally balanced animal feeds. In addition, the increasing use of light and temperature-controlled housing [help stimulate] growth and reproduction.''

With the publication in 1964 in Great Britain of Ruth Harrison's book, *Animal Machines,* concern for the welfare of farm animals grew. Ms. Harrison coined the expression "factory farming" to indicate she thought meat and dairy producers treated their livestock and poultry as machines that could be intensively used to produce food without regard to their well-being. This caused the animals untold, needless suffering and had potentially damaging effects on their food as well.

Today, we have two distinct camps: Animal rights advocates are concerned about preventing needless suffering of livestock and poultry; the producers of meat, dairy products, and eggs, whose primary motive is production for profit, stand on the opposing side of the issue.

Somewhere in the middle are the animal scientists, who are now investigating how animal food production can be made more efficient and less costly, but who are at the same time equally concerned for the welfare of the creatures being reared for food.

II. *Pros and Cons Of Factory Farming*

A. *Animal Rights Activists*

Advocates of animal rights are concerned about the welfare of animals being reared for foodstuffs. As People for the Ethical Treatment of Animals (PETA) has charged, "the factory farming system of modern agriculture strives to produce the most meat, milk, and eggs as quickly and cheaply as possible and in the smallest space possible. Cows, calves, pigs, chickens, turkeys, ducks, geese, rabbits, and other animals are kept in cages or stalls so small they are often unable to turn around. They are deprived of exercise so that all their bodies' energy goes toward producing flesh for human consumption and other by-products. They are fed growth hormones to fatten them fast and are genetically altered to grow larger or to produce more milk and eggs than nature originally intended.''

Michael Fox, veterinarian and animal scientist for the Humane Society of the United States (HSUS), has written extensively on animals who suffer in factory farms. In his 1981 report for the HSUS, Fox documents some of the major shortcomings in current animal husbandry practices. Fox says his report is still valid more than a decade later, because those responsible for factory farming have not complied with needed reforms. These are some of the salient points in Fox's report:

1. Stress and suffering are standard fare for animals living on factory farms, because farms are overstocked and provided with inadequate veterinary care. Good animal husbandry has been replaced by such questionable practices as administering drugs to prevent certain illnesses—illnesses most often created by bad husbandry in the first place! And with too many animals to look after, the sick ones are rarely noticed; when they are, it's often too late or costly and time-consuming to treat them.

2. In factory farms, severe physical restriction is commonplace. Animals crowded in small pens or battery cages or tethered in separate stalls cannot even perform simple motions such as grooming, preening, stretching, turning, and lying down.

3. Many feed-lot beef and dairy cattle are rarely provided with shade or shelter. With concentrated diets, they also become more susceptible to extremes in

temperature. On the other hand, if cattle were free to roam on the range or in pastures, they would naturally seek shade or shelter when available and needed.

· 4. Some producers claim that animals have a more peaceful life when confined to controlled, indoor environments than they would outside, exposed to rivals and predators. Even if this were true for some farms, the argument is fallacious. While tethered sows don't risk injury from fighting, as they might if they were kept in yards, fighting occurs most often when yards and pens are overstocked. Fighting may be a symptom of bad husbandry, but keeping sows tied down or penned alone all their lives is also not a humane solution.

5. In a state of confined helplessness, these animals are wholly dependent upon men and machines. And with the increased complexity in machines that provide food and water for the animals, it is not infrequent that these systems break down and fail to provide for the animals' most basic needs.

6. Farm animals are subjected to continuous, unnecessary physical pain and suffering. Branding of cattle, castration of bulls, and dehorning are usually done without any kind of anesthetic. Pigs often have their tails cut off to avoid injuries from companions; however, because of confined quarters, pigs tend to bite one another's ears and shoulders instead.

7. With accelerated growth and production in factory farming, animals are too often pushed beyond normal, humane limits to produce milk, meat, and eggs. Hogs, dairy cows, laying hens, and broiler chickens suffer from a number of production-induced diseases, just because they are forced to exceed their limits of tolerance to meet production targets.

B. *Claims of the Animal Husbandry Industry*
Spokespersons for the animal husbandry industry

charge that animal rights activists vastly exaggerate the inhumane rearing conditions for livestock and poultry on factory farms. Steve Kopperud, Executive Director of the Animal Industry Foundation, maintains that "one of the strongholds of animal welfare in our culture is the farmer. With the exception of zoos and animal parks, only the farmer enjoys close daily contact with animals. As farmers tend livestock and poultry, guaranteeing their health and welfare, the animals provide an economic return to the farmer in the form of wholesome, high quality foods valued by the vast majority of consumers."

The Foundation's brochure called, "Animal Agriculture—Myths and Facts," is valuable to animal rights activists, because it states succinctly many of the views of those who produce and market the products of cattle and poultry, including the following selected statements:

• Animals have no rights.

• Farmers and ranchers are neither cruel nor naive.

• Farming in our country is not dominated by huge agribusinesses but is still in the hands of family farmers.

• Producers still prefer to keep animals in barns rather than in factory farms, with the exception of beef cattle, where confinement is used to protect the animal.

• It is a myth that animals are so confined in crates and cages that they cannot move at all. Where restraints are used, they are designed for the welfare of the animals as well as in the interests of production efficiency.

• It is a gross overstatement that farm animals are routinely and unnecessarily mutilated by beak trimming, tail docking, branding, dehorning, castration, and other inhumane practices. These practices are conducted in a professional manner to ensure the welfare of the animals.

• It is false to claim that farm animals in confinement are prone to disease, thus forcing farmers to routinely use antibiotics, hormones, and other drugs to keep the animals alive. In fact, animals in confinement are generally healthier because they are protected.

C. *Science Tries To Help*

Somewhere in between the positions of animal rights advocates and the food animal producers are those of animal scientists who wish to establish more humane practices in the production, transit, slaughter, and marketing of animals for food and other by-products. In a 1981 report entitled, "Scientific Aspects of the Welfare of Food Animals," issued by the Council for Agricultural Science and Technology, the welfare of poultry, swine, cattle, and sheep is evaluated at each step in production, transportation, and slaughter.

The report identified two broad classes of concern for the welfare of food animals: (1) that the practices employed be suitable for achieving the purposes for which the animals have been maintained, and (2) that the practices recognize the nature of domestic animals as perceptive, sensitive, living beings.

Without criticizing animal growers, the report discusses, among other things:

• How artificial light, temperature, air pollutants such as ammonia, ventilation, beak trimming, removal of combs, wing and toe clipping, and induced molting in poultry are influenced by production needs of flesh and eggs.

• How floor space, lighting, flooring, stalls or crates, straw bedding, grooming, tail removal, castration, and disease influence production of swine for meat and other products.

• How housing and space needs, temperature control, caging and crating, feedlot practices, and health protection affect beef cattle, dairy cows, veal calves, and sheep produced for flesh and other products.

• How animals are handled, transported, and slaughtered. The report at no time recommends eliminating inhumane practices, although it does identify the scientific research and management practices currently being practiced by animal scientists and producers of animal foods.

III. *The Official Policy Of The National Humane Education Society*

Our Society believes farmers and ranchers producing animal flesh and other products, handlers and transporters of animals, and slaughterhouses all have a moral obligation to maintain humane production practices to the greatest extent possible. The Society also believes consumers must express their concern—and vote with their pocketbooks—so that animals will be cared for and dispatched most humanely.

We believe, for example, that a vegetarian diet is preferable from two standpoints: it both enhances the health of humans, and it spares animals from inhumane practices in growing, and slaughtering. Of course, the goal of turning all meat-eating humans into vegetarians is not attainable in the near future; the least we can expect for now is that all animals are treated as humanely as possible.

The needs of animals that should be addressed include: (1) providing adequate space for exercising and meeting other basic needs, (2) building shelters and other housing to protect animals from abrupt temperature changes, (3) maintaining adequate light and darkness in daily operations, (4) protecting animals from stress due to close quarters and lengthy artificial daylight, and (5) limiting how much each animal can reasonably produce without stretching their limits and treating them inhumanely.

IV. *Conclusion*

Despite scientific advances that have been made concerning animal welfare, some farmers and ranchers, some transporters of live animals, and some slaughterhouses still maintain inhumane management practices. The goal of all Americans, including consumers and producers, should be the elimination of needless, preventable suffering of animals.

A vegetarian diet most definitely helps eliminate animal suffering, since the diet does not require the flesh and other products of agricultural animals. However, short of having all people adopt such a diet, we encourage consumers to minimize the amount of animal products they buy. With less demand for animal products, fewer animals will be subjected to needless, inhumane suffering to meet insane production targets.

CHAPTER X

Illegal Dogfighting: Barbarism At Its Worst

It's hard to say why people like to watch dogs fight to the finish. The blood, gore, and senseless death are enough to make most people sick—but not the thousands upon thousands of humans who use dogs either to make money, to bolster their own egos or prestige, or just to give their own thirst for blood and revenge a "safe outlet."

Well, it's certainly not safe for the dogs. And I'm not sure what there is in it for them, either. But, because human beings continue to practice this abomination in the name of "sport," we still allow dogs to be forced into cruel, senseless fights, even though these contests are illegal throughout the United States.

I. *The Origins of Dogfighting*

The blood sport of dogfighting goes back thousands of years, when uncivilized humans pitted their domesticated dogs against those of other owners. These early humans probably took pride in the fact that some of their dogs fought courageously and won in contests with other canines. Contests were waged in many parts of the world, and colonists brought the dogs to America from Great Britain and continental European countries.

Today, dogfighting is banned in Europe and the United States. More than half of the states in the U.S. have passed laws making it a felony to wage such events. In some states, it is even a felony to watch the contests. Enforcement falls under the federal Animal Welfare Act.

In dogfighting as it is known and practiced illegally today, owners prefer pit bull terriers bred for fighting spirit. Special training makes the dogs engage in savage bloody attacks, often resulting in the death of the losing contestant and serious wounding of the winner. In clandestine arenas, a select number of spectators, secretly informed of the contest, join in watching the dogs fight until one or both animals are so injured and exhausted they cannot go on. Gambling is a large part of the contests, as owners and spectators wage substantial amounts of money on each of the participating animals.

II. *Profile Of The Contestants And Their Owners*

Alexandra Rockey, who published an article on dogfighting in *Police Product News* magazine, classifies dogfight owners and fanciers as follows:

1. Serious owners, estimated to total at least 10,000, who take great pride in breeding, training, and fighting their canines;

2. Several thousand hobbyists and fanciers who frequently witness such contests and place money bets; and

3. Several thousand street fighters who encourage their dogs to fight to win respect for their masters in their neighborhoods.

A typical contest is described in the following account of a raid. Rockey reported on "a noted Arkansas raid as a result of long-term work with an informant who often was told about such events. Two hundred fifty spectators and owners were arrested at the scene, where these people gathered, coming from nine states. The total amount of money expropriated at the arena was about half a million dollars. Sixty-nine concealed handguns were confiscated, as well as significant amounts of narcotics. Participating agencies included the Arkansas State Police, the FBI, the U.S. Department of Agriculture, the Humane Society of the United States (HSUS), and the Organized Crime Task Forces from Arkansas and Tennessee. The action resulted in the first convictions ever under the federal Animal Welfare Act.''

The fighting pit bulls, which weigh from 30 to 60 pounds, have jaws of exceptional strength, and a wide chest and box-like head, would be quite attractive if they were not bred and trained to be killers. This kind of dogfighting requires animals to be predisposed seriously to attack each other, something that is unnatural among dogs in the wild. Wild dogs fight one another to establish dominance and mastery over harems, but the contests never end with grave injuries. One of the fighters simply withdraws and thereby indicates he is the loser.

In the arenas, however, the inhibition against fighting to the bitter end has been bred out, and this, coupled with special training, contribute to the pit bulls' savage attacks, which often result in the death of the loser.

As an editorial in an underground dogfighting publications states, ''They call us criminals for allowing an even-weight contest between two willing animals to take place, and our rules don't read, 'kill or be killed.' Our rules simply mean fight if you want, quit if you want, and in between we'll see that you get a fair chance.''

III. *Why This Blood Sport Should Continue To Be Banned*

Stephen Torre, Director of the Law Enforcement Department for the Massachusetts Society for the Prevention of Cruelty to Animals, has been following this blood sport for a number of years. He believes dogfighting should continue to be banned in all 50 states under the provisions of the Animal Welfare Act. Dogfight promoters may refer to their sadistic pastime as a sport, but the blood-spattered bodies of combatants speak against the contests as a humane sport.

A *Close-Up Report* entitled "Dogfighters on the Run," published by the Humane Society of the United States (HSUS), contains the following:

> "Words alone—no matter how descriptive— cannot adequately portray the sickening reality of dogfighting. The sounds, the smells, the unforgettable sights of this degrading, bizarre spectacle are enough to revolt all but the most degenerate members of the human race. How can anyone derive satisfaction from watching two dogs tear each other apart? How can anyone sit for hours, not only watching, but cheering every wound, broken leg, and mangled eye."

A typical dogfight unfolds in the following manner: Fighting canines are held in corners of the pit of the arena. When the referee shouts "face your dogs," the animals are placed in opposite corners. After the words "let go the terriers" are heard, the canines attack each other. Each seeks to lock onto the body of the antagonist, and there is no escape. The powerful force of the jaws often cannot be shaken off by the victim. The dog with the more powerful jaw holds, tears, and shakes the competitor, and blood and urine splatter the arena pit. Despite serious injuries incurred early in the fight—puncture wounds, large gashes, broken bones, and internal injuries—the canines continue to grapple until one or both collapse or are dragged exhausted out of the pit.

The inhumane suffering, however, is not confined to the arenas. As Torre indicates, the road to becoming a fighter is fraught with cruelties. In training from the puppy stage to adulthood, dogs are encouraged to whet their appetites for blood. Kittens and other live creatures are dangled in front of their faces, and the dogs are egged on to kill the live bait brutally and mercilessly. Puppies and meek dogs adopted from pounds and shelters often serve as lures for fighters-in-training.

The HSUS report indicates why such contests continue and often elude law enforcement agents. ''For years the underground network of dogfighters—with devotees in virtually every state and social stratum—has gone to extremes to keep its activities tightly under wraps. In fact, so cautious are fight organizers that until the last possible moment, even attendees are kept in the dark as to the fight's whereabouts. Only minutes before a fight is scheduled to begin are patrons rounded up from various obscure meeting places and convoyed to the site. There they go through a series of security checks, and once inside, no one is permitted to leave until the fights are over for fear authorities will be tipped off.''

IV. *The Official Policy Of The National Humane Education Society*

Commendably, in every state, law enforcement agencies are now poised to apprehend promoters and spectators of dogfights and to prosecute them. Cooperative efforts between the enforcement officials and representatives of humane societies are paying off. Law enforcement people follow up on humane activists' leads and frequent arrests are made. Penalties upon conviction include jail terms and fines, and the evidence shows these penalties have deterred many persons from breaking the law against dogfighting.

Of course, in the meantime, pet bull terriers still suffer a bad reputation because they are preferred in dogfights. However, when properly reared and trained, these canines can be as gentle and loving as beagles.

Our Society therefore believes:

1. Fights among pit bulls and other dogs promoted by human beings should continue to be banned as inhumane.

2. Promoters and spectators of such barbaric, savage contests should be apprehended, tried, and punished if convicted.

Humane societies can and should assist the law enforcement community by learning where such events are held and passing this information on to the officers. As with the apprehension of all criminals, cooperative citizens can go far to eliminate evil practices by assisting law enforcement agents in seizing transgressors.

3. Children and adults should be educated to consider such contests atrocious and not worth watching.

4. Pit bull terriers bred and trained to attack are extremely dangerous, but others can be reared with care from the puppy stage and will not be a threat to anyone. Not all pit bull terriers therefore should be considered dangerous. In all attacks against humans and other animals, evidence reveals that the offending dogs were improperly trained and should be impounded and euthanized humanely.

5. We must steadfastly reject the arguments by promoters and spectators that, because other cruel, inhumane sports such as cockfighting are legal, dogfighting should be legalized.

6. All humane societies should dedicate themselves to educating the public to shun cruel sports involving animals. Modern-day humans have the opportunity to view many outdoor and indoor sports that are not inhumane but just as satisfying. Whatever justifications our distant ancestors had for dogfighting have long ago disappeared; today, this inhumane contest is no longer acceptable.

CHAPTER XI

Cockfighting—
Down And Dirty

Unlike dogfighting, cockfighting is still legal in Puerto Rico and four states: Arizona, New Mexico, Louisiana, and Oklahoma. Like dogfighting, though, it is a cruel and unusual blood sport that deserves to be banned everywhere, for all time.

I. *Nature and Origin of Cockfighting*

Cockfighting pits specially bred and armed roosters to fight each other to the death. It is conducted in small arenas with dirt floors and walls separating contestants from spectators.

The "sport," as its devotees like call it, goes as far back into antiquity as historians can trace. Ancient India and Persia had such events, which then spread westward to Greece and Rome, and eastward to China and Indochina. The Phoenicians reportedly brought the contests to Britain, and the English then introduced cockfighting to the New World.

The popularity of these contests seems to have come from the pleasure many people experience in witnessing bloody events. At the same time, however, some sensitive people have objected to the contests—witness the fact that, by 1834, cockfights were banned in Great Britain. In the United States, the contests were popular up to the early 20th century, at which time individual states began banning cockfighting. Today, all but Puerto Rico and the four states named above have made the contests illegal. In many states, it is even illegal to witness cockfights.

Laws have become more and more stringent, to the point where cockfighting now often leads to felonious charges and court cases. Of course, illegal contests still persist, because purses for winning roosters and spectators' bets more than offset the risks involved in participating in cockfights.

II. *A Typical Cockfight*

Gamecock handlers provoke the roosters by first thrusting them at one other. The birds are then thrown into the ring for the fight, which often ends in the death of one contestant and the severe injuring of the "victor."

The gamecocks are armed with steel gaffs as sharp as icepicks, which make it possible for the birds to severely and painfully injure each other. The roosters gouge out eyes, tear open breasts, puncture lungs, break bones in wings and legs, and pierce skulls.

Contests often go beyond the usual 10- to 15-minute attacks, in which cases the birds are removed to side pits where they are induced to finish the contest by killing or gravely injuring one another. In a so-called "battle royal," surviving injured birds are tossed into the ring to see who will be the ultimate winner.

There are still those who champion these contests as legitimate sporting events. More sensitive, caring persons are struggling to bring a halt to the contests throughout the country.

III. *Arguments For And Against Cockfights*

A. *Arguments For*

By vocation, Joe Zannino is a funeral director. By avocation, however, he is a gamecock breeder who takes his birds to arenas in Arizona, Louisiana, and Puerto

Rico. Zannino is also a spokesperson for the United Gamebird Breeders Association (UGBA), a 15,000-member group that supports the breeding of gamecocks.

Zannino is not apologetic about his avocation: "Hunting, fishing, and fox hunting are considered by many persons to be acceptable sporting events. The same is true about cockfighting. Our sport, however, is based on the natural tendency in roosters to fight each other. In hunting, fishing, and fox hunting, the animals are not natural enemies of each other. They are taken by people without desire in the animals to compete."

In cockfighting, owners seek to equalize the factors—age, weight, and steel gaffs—that otherwise would make the contest unfair. Zanino explains that "witnessing the events firsthand gives one the pleasure to see how heroic the roosters are, as well as their stamina and fighting spirit. Bravery is valued by people in all creatures, and roosters more than many other animals are brave fighters determined to establish their superiority."

Zanino adds that, whereas the roosters fight one another, they are not hostile toward hens and other creatures, including man. As long as they are not provoked, they can be handled and petted without injury to the hand of the person touching them.

Zanino argues that, with the exception of hunting and fishing, no other sport has been so long and so universally accepted by people in all walks of life as has cockfighting. Ask any cockfight promoter about the fighting spirit of gamecocks, and he will say it comes from careful breeding of the creatures over the past several thousand years. Special training and conditioning add to the rooster's ability to compete against others.

"Special breeding," Zannino points out, "is why 15,000 of us have banned together in the UGBA. We want the superior hereditary lines to continue so that the gamecocks do not deteriorate in mating. Just as horses have superior blood lines, we of UGBA believe gamecocks have superior traits that are passed on in careful mating to new generations of fighting roosters."

Superior fighters that recover from wounds derived in combat are candidates for breeding new generations of fighters. Zanino indicates that breeding gamecocks doesn't require large outlays: "I have fifty gamecocks doing nicely on a couple of acres of land. A gamebird breeder, however, must be prepared to separate roosters from each other after a little more than a half a year since birth to prevent their natural tendency to fight each other."

Zannino asks, "What other sport that doesn't include doping and other bad practices is there like cockfighting? Artificial spurs given to the roosters have been criticized as inhumane, but they speed up combats and thus reduce the time the gamebirds suffer in the rings. On the other hand, in hunting, many animals are wounded and escape with wounds causing long-time suffering."

B. *Arguments Against*
Robert Baker, investigator for the Humane Society of the United States, has been evaluating cockfights for more than eight years. The more he witnesses these contests, "the more convinced I become that they should be totally banned in all 50 states and Puerto Rico."

Why the negative impression? Baker says that the contests, "which I refuse to call a sport, are inherently inhumane. People who like the contests say they are no more cruel than hunting, fishing, and fox hunting, but I challenge the notion that any hunters or fishermen let animals sought after suffer for sometimes even several hours with painful injuries. I know no hunter or angler who takes pleasure in allowing the quarry to suffer at some length unnecessarily."

Whatever aggression the roosters have toward each other results from breeding and training rather than some "natural" fighting urge. As Baker points out, "people whose roosters are fighting will not let the birds retreat. Indeed, to incite aggression, owners toss their birds at each other until they respond by fighting."

In addition, Baker attests that many birds are drugged so they will become excited. Where contestants do not kill or gravely injure one another, special contests ("battle royals") at the end of the evening are arranged in separate pits so injured, surviving birds can "finish off" one another no matter how long it takes. Are gamecocks braver than other creatures? Baker cites abundant research which shows that when creatures are forced to fight, they will protect themselves by attacking their tormentors. It's ludicrous to call gamecocks "brave" in a completely unnatural situation where they are egged on to be violent and aggressive.

Baker is often asked what particular aspect of the contests is most inhumane. His answer: "sustained suffering for very painful injuries resulting from attacks that do not immediately lead to death and thus are painfully lingering." It is not uncommon for gamecocks to attack one other for up to two hours. The roosters suffer from a gouged-out eye, a punctured breast, or a skull pierced by the gaffs.

"Those of us in the humane movement," says Baker, "must continue to press for bans on all cockfights in all the states, and to make the penalties for participating and witnessing such barbarous contests more severe. We must continue to work for more enforcement of existing laws because cockfighting now takes place sometimes even in states where the contests are illegal."

IV. *The Official Policy of the National Humane Education Society*

Our Society agrees with Robert Baker concerning cruel, bloody cockfighting. Certainly, to call such barbarism a "sport" is highly objectionable, and to liken cockfighting to hunting, fishing, and fox hunting is absurd. Even if cockfighting were like these outdoor practices, the contests would still be objectionable—because many aspects of hunting and fishing are also inhumane!

Our Society's official policy therefore is as follows:

1. Cockfighting is not a decent outdoor sport and doesn't deserve spectators. Fighting by gamecocks to gravely injure and even kill opponents is barbaric, grossly inhumane, and should be universally outlawed.

2. Witnessing such bloody contests desensitizes spectators and makes them prone to behave cruelly to animals and other humans. People should get their thrills from truly humane contests such as soccer, tennis, golf, track, baseball, and other spectator sports.

3. Roosters participating in cockfights are bred, trained, and drugged to be aggressive. Their "bravery" is a sham.

4. Roosters deserve to be bred for their natural role, as protectors of harems of hens that mate with these males.

5. We need laws banning such barbarisms where they are still legal—in Arizona, Louisiana, New Mexico, Oklahoma and Puerto Rico. In states that currently ban cockfighting, we need greater enforcement to prevent illegal contests from being held.

6. Illegal cockfighting should carry severe punishments, as severe as those handed out for felonies. In other words, it should be a felony to stage and witness such cruel contests.

V. Conclusion

Cockfighting is not a true sport and should be banned everywhere. Breeding, conditioning, and drugging the roosters to be aggressive are unacceptable, grossly inhumane practices. It is even objectionable to witness and cheer such contests.

Despite the fact that, in the past, emperors and kings enjoyed witnessing these bloody events, these "traditions" cannot be called anything other than brutally inhumane practices. Many bad practices were tolerated for centuries (like slavery), but then abolished when reasonable opposition to the practices escalated and prevailed. It is imperative that we educate people in all walks of life to the ethical principle that long-term barbarisms are no longer acceptable—regardless of how long they have been practiced.

CHAPTER XII

The Good And The Bad About Thoroughbred Racing

Early humans prized horses for their food. Around the Stone Age, humans began to domesticate the larger horses that were evolving. Being slow in comparison to many animals, people found they could gain an advantage of speed by riding horses.

Soon after the domestication of horses, humans learned to breed horses for valued traits such as speed, stamina, sturdiness, and hardiness. One of the earliest written accounts of horse breeding in what is now Turkey dates back to 1500 B.C. Throughout recorded times, horses have served human masters in war, farming, transport, recreation, and uses such as racing.

I. *The Origin of Horse Racing*

Horse racing probably arose as a diversion among early peoples soon after horses were domesticated. Thoroughbred racing as we know it probably began in Britain around the Renaissance. From the outset, it was considered a sport of kings.

In the era of Charles II, the art of intensive selective horse breeding for qualities valued in racing was established. The Jockey Club, founded in England around 1790, formalized regulations for breeding and registering thoroughbreds and the conditions under which they could be raced. Jockey Clubs soon spread to many other countries.

Racing came to North America from England, brought by people seeking refuge and favorable opportunities for the sport in the 18th century. Today in the United States, we have steeple chases, trotting contests, quarterhorse running, and thoroughbred racing. Thoroughbred racing has been the most popular of these events in our country.

In 1988, about 55 million people attended horse races in the 43 states which have legal provisions permitting parimutuel racing (not all states have tracks even if they sanction them). Over 90,000 horses race at the 84 tracks in operation.

The question remains, however, whether this sport is humane for the horses themselves. Some say yes, others say no.

II. *Reasons For And Against The Sport*

A. *Reasons For*

Howard Bass, spokesperson for Thoroughbred Racing Communications Inc., a group that follows the sport, says the thoroughbred industry is humane and a valued contributor to the economy. He estimates that racing contributes more than $20 billion annually to the economy. About $9 billion of this comes from betting, and some $670 million are won annually in purses.

Bass states, however, that "economics is not the main reason for thoroughbred racing. Many horse owners—although mindful and governed by expenses to care for the animals—are mainly interested in seeing the horses run and win. Very few owners make a good living by the purses that are won by their horses. Their primary interest is love of the sport."

According to Bass, the typical horse owner has a stable for his horses but is not particularly wealthy. Expenses for housing, feeding, medically treating, and training the horses govern how often owners can race their horses. Given these expenses, most horse owners show little or no profit from winning race purses.

The average length of time each horse races is about eight years. However, Bass says only a fraction of thoroughbreds have full racing careers. Those that do not run well and others whose racing days are over are disposed of humanely. Some wind up on farms and in neighborhood stables as pets in the suburbs, others perform in horse shows. A few are slaughtered for food.

Bass discounts claims of widespread doping of race horses as greatly exaggerated. He says that veterinarians routinely check for possible doping, as this is required by the states. Of course, a few unscrupulous trainers succeed in getting away with doping despite the checks, but for the most part, horses are given only substances that are medically acceptable and legal.

Bass says that injuries are promptly treated where and when horses can be cared for humanely. Veterinarians give lethal doses only to injured horses that they deem will not recover. Since owners stand to lose their investment if the horses are put to death, there is a built-in incentive to keep injured horses alive and restore them back to full health.

Horses with good conformation and excellent racing skills often wind up as sires and breeders of thoroughbreds. They are cared for expertly and are given pastures and stables, because owners and buyers value their offspring. Geldings are castrated and cannot mate, so their ultimate disposition is to other horse lovers and to slaughterhouses.

Bass admits truth in the critics' protest that horses begin to race when they are still too young—usually at the age of two, even though the horses' bones are not yet fully mature. Because the horses are expensive to raise and train, owners feel pressed to race young horses as soon as they are able.

The total number of horses or jockeys lost due to injury is not available. However, Bass admits the sport is dangerous. "No matter how careful or skillful jockeys are in completing races, accidents can and do happen," Bass says.

In addition, horses that are on a winning streak are raced as often as possible, regardless of bad weather or bad track conditions. Particularly if the horse tolerates rain, cold, and heat easily, the horse is run continuously. Likewise, the hard, cracked surfaces of some tracks in cold weather take their toll, as do wet, muddy tracks.

Bass concludes, "despite the shortcomings, thoroughbred racing is humane and will likely continue indefinitely. I would not support such racing if inhumane conditions were prevalent in the industry. But it is a rare thrill to see horses compete fairly under equal conditions to win for their owners."

B. *Reasons Against*

Robert Baker of the Humane Society of the United States has been following thoroughbred racing for more than 10 years. He has a decidedly negative impression about thoroughbred racing as it is practiced today.

Why object to thoroughbred racing? Baker acknowledges that, under ideal conditions, the sport could be pleasant for both horse and spectator. But parimutuel racing exploits horses to gratify horse owners, trainers, track veterinarians, and racetrack operators, as well as the state regulators standing to add revenues to treasuries. It is therefore an inhumane sport.

This exploitation results in the tragic death of thousands of thoroughbreds each year and the abuse of thousands of others.

Baker feels strongly that racing horses when they are still young is the most inhumane practice of all. At two years of age, skeletal and muscular systems in the horses are not fully mature or resilient enough to withstand the punishment of racing. This results in many short-term and lifelong injuries. According to Baker, the American Association of Equine Practitioners lists two-year-old racing as a major cause of injuries to racehorses.

Baker also charges that it is cruel and inhumane to race horses as often as possible for the sake of profit, thereby ignoring the physical condition or fatigue of the horses.

Then there is the problem of faulty racetrack surfaces. Baker's investigations revealed that "many track surfaces are kept intentionally hard to provide fast race times. Hard surfaces are conducive to extreme concussion to the horses' limbs, resulting in many horses becoming lame."

It goes without saying that horses are often raced in inclement weather and in extremes of heat and cold, because canceling a race would result in too great a loss of revenue.

On top of all these problems, there is abusive, illegal drugging of horses, in order to force them onto the track. Although states require veterinarians to test for drugs after races, unscrupulous trainers get away with the practice because the tests often fail to indicate the presence of illegal drugs.

Painkilling drugs will mask a horse's pain, enabling the creature to run as fast as it can, even with an injured leg. Such a practice, however, aggravates injuries and often causes spills from which the animal is severely crippled and must be destroyed. Some bone-breaking spills even result in pileups of horses falling on one another, trampling other horses and jockeys.

Baker says "veterinarians estimate 80% of racehorses have some kind of injury, especially joint damage and joint disease."

Thoroughbred racing advocates often claim that the large revenues generated by the sport justify the cruelties and excesses. Baker objects that this "is a hideous argument. No amount of money should be reason for inhumane practices."

But it is clear that money rules over any sense of ethics when it comes to horseracing. In Baker's own words: "As long as the competition is a business and not wholly a sport, money will always be mentioned as an argument in behalf of the event, regardless of the condition of the horses. Because of the large amounts of money wagered at the tracks, the potential for huge profits is there, and the likelihood of abolishing such events is rather nebulous. And so I believe the sport is here to stay."

How can owners in good conscience allow their horses to be mistreated? Baker responds, "Horses are only valuable to owners if the creatures are racing and winning purses. Regardless of a horse being tired, ill, or injured, owners are reluctant to rest a horse because then the animal is not making money. And failure to make money forces the owner to dispose of the horse, whether to a farm or a neighborhood stable. Most often, the end of these creatures is the slaughterhouse."

Even if we cannot abolish the sport, as Baker believes, we must constantly raise objections to inhumane conditions at the stables and racetracks. Our local, state, and federal legislators should be constantly reminded that terrible inhumane practices are crying out for remedial legislative measures.

III. *The Official Policy of the National Humane Education Society*

Like Robert Baker, we agree it is unlikely that thoroughbred racing will or can be abolished. But we also accept his view that pressure should be put on our local, state, and federal legislators to take note of the inhumane practices and conditions that prevail in the sport as we now know it.

The following inhumane conditions and practices make clear the official policy of the National Humane Education Society on thoroughbred racing:

1. Thoroughbreds are introduced to racing at too early an age, when their skeletal and muscular systems are still immature. Holding off racing until the horses are four or five would prevent a number of lifelong injuries caused by racing at two years. However, this change may never happen, because of the lucrative races specifically for two- and three-year-olds, including the Kentucky Derby, Pimlico, and Belmont races. We should not give up trying to force owners and trainers to forego these competitions until thoroughbreds are more mature.

2. Hard surfaces at the tracks should be eliminated because of the toll exacted on horses. Softer surfaces prevent injuries even though they slow down speeds.

3. More time off from racing is needed. Rest periods, especially during extreme cold and heat, are essential. The periods between races should also be lengthened.

4. Doping by unscrupulous trainers must be eliminated. Since present tests sometimes fail to uncover the presence of illicit drugs in the horse, better tests are needed. The result would be fewer injuries and longer racing careers for most thoroughbreds.

5. Treatment of existing injuries and diseases is absolutely essential. Owners must be persuaded not to simply "give up" on thoroughbreds that cannot race because of disabling conditions. If owners cannot afford the extra treatment, they should not be in the business of racing.

6. Owners must also make greater efforts to find good homes for the horses that cannot race any longer. More sanctuaries are needed like the Thoroughbred Retirement Foundation in New York State. Owners should

lead the way in establishing more of these homes throughout the country.

IV. *Conclusion*

Thoroughbred racing should be recognized as a sport *only if* these deficiencies are rectified. As it exists today, the competition is primarily a business, with far too much emphasis placed on amassing large profits. Properly regulated and administered, thoroughbred racing could be a humane, highly popular sport both for the horses and for the millions of spectators who enjoy a "day at the races."

CHAPTER XIII

Wild Birds Make Endangered Pets!

They're stunning to look at. They've got bright, colorful plumage. They make pretty noises.

And they "adorn" many households in the most highly civilized parts of the world—Europe, Japan, and the United States.

Who are "they"?

They're exotic birds, and they make deadly pets. Not because they harm their owners, but because, by purchasing these pets, human beings are assuring the virtual destruction of many species of wild birds.

Some of the victims—which hail from Africa, Central and South America, and Asia—include the scarlet, hyacinth, red-fronted and Spix's macaws, yellow-headed and red-crowned amazons, and the palm and salmon-crested cockatoos. These and many other birds have become seriously endangered, both because their habitats have been destroyed and because they have been captured for sale as pets.

How serious is the situation? Well, it is estimated that 1,000 of the existing 8,700 bird species will face certain extinction, unless their capture and the destruction of their habitat are not restricted—immediately.

As many as 20 million birds, including many beautiful parrots, are caught each year and sold as pets. The tragedy is compounded by the fact that nearly half the birds die as they are captured, and one-third of those that survive capture perish in holding points and during transport.

That's why we at the Society raise three cheers for the International Union for the Conservation of Nature and Natural Resources (IUCN)! This group adopted a resolution urging all nations to greatly restrict the capture and trade of wild birds. Representing government agencies and private groups from 120 nations around the world, the IUCN adopted this resolution out of concern for the rapid worldwide decline in many wild bird species. As an organization that has repeatedly been effective in its efforts to save the world's natural resources, the IUCN has the track record to have an impact on this crisis situation.

The Defenders of Wildlife should also be congratulated for its role in placing the draft resolution on IUCN's agenda and winning majority support for this initiative. Special thanks go to Jim Wyerman of the Defenders of Wildlife, who wrote the draft resolution and shepherded it through the various stages on the way to adoption.

I. *Flight of Doom*

By demanding to have exotic birds as pets, Europeans, Americans, and the Japanese are responsible for hastening the extinction of many species of wild birds.

Just how big the scope of the problem is can be illustrated with a few examples: In 1987, Belgium imported about 105,000 birds of endangered and threatened species; Belgian authorities received applications to import nearly half a million birds—more than all the legal imports in the United States in 1988.

In the Netherlands, nearly 138,000 birds of species threatened with extinction were imported in 1987; in Germany, 30,000 parrots were imported, about twice as many as were shipped to any other European country. The previous year, France granted licenses to import 4.8 million birds.

According to Peter Knights, an official of the Environmental Investigation Agency, a private, British-based group studying the wild bird trade in Europe, these birds are subject to horrendous conditions upon their capture.

"In Senegal (Africa), captured birds are gathered up for weekly deliveries in cages containing as many as 2,000 creatures. They are then picked up by an agent in the capital, Dakar. After trips of up to 400 miles, often in stifling heat, the surviving birds are unloaded into modest sized aviaries at the exporter's quarters," Knights explains.

"The capture and transport to exporters' quarters take a terrible toll, but there are also disastrous mortality rates aboard overseas air transport. So, what started out as unacceptably high death rates in capture and traffic to exporting quarters are multiplied in air transit to facilities of importing nations."

II. *Traffic In Death*

Most of the birds that die in transit die from excessive heat or cold, deprivation of food and water, crowding, or epidemic diseases.

"Spokesmen for the pet trade have argued for many years that the death rate in air transit and in quarantine at points of entry is low," Knights says. "But study after study shows that this is not the whole story."

For instance, a British report released in 1989 noted that, from a survey of 12 European nations, an average of 14% of birds were dead on arrival or died during the five-week quarantine period. A closer look at the data reveals just how devastating commercial air travel is for wild birds: dead on arrival in the Netherlands: 17%; in

Germany: 27%; and in Denmark, as many as 33% of parrots did not survive the journey. The list goes on and on.

Faced with such staggering losses, leading European airlines such as Lufthansa are rethinking and even abandoning the transport of wild birds, Knights reports. "The public reaction to the mind-boggling mortality rate is having a positive effect on airline executives fearful of a loss of business by passengers who are becoming aware of the great tragedy of bird losses."

Environmentalists also blame U.S. authorities for inadequate inspection of imports and illegal trafficking of birds in this country. It is estimated that 1.3 million of the 6.5 million birds imported into the U.S. between 1980 and 1988 perished *en route*.

Upwards of 100,000 of these birds came from endangered species and were smuggled into the country. Drugged, gagged, and crammed into tiny recesses of cars and trucks, or floated in cages across the Rio Grande from Mexico, these birds are at greater risk than legally imported birds, since they have not been examined or quarantined to determine if they are disease-free. Of course, not only does it endanger the health of the birds themselves, it also poses a serious threat to domestic flocks, including millions of chickens and turkeys.

III. *Import Bans: A Long Way To Go*

One hundred and eight nations have agreed to ban the sale of endangered species through the Convention on International Trade in Endangered Species of Wild Fauna and Flora (CITES). That seems like tremendous progress, but this number can be somewhat misleading, particularly since many countries lack the resources or commitment to properly enforce the ban and effectively protect endangered birds.

Even in the United States, for instance, enforcement has its limitations. While the Joint Fish and Wildlife Advisory Service (JFWAT) has the authority to inspect imports to determine if they include endangered species, agency staff lament that the office is crippled by insufficient funding and too few inspectors. In addition, sources at JFWAT report that the permit system that allows other countries to export birds and animals to the U.S. is woefully inadequate. Issuing countries often lack precise data on which birds are banned on the CITES list, leading to the inadvertent capture and sale of many wild birds of endangered species.

Further stacking the deck against effective enforcement is the fact that some countries involved in the CITES Convention have not yet established proper inspection at their exporting facilities. So we still have a long way to go in making sure endangered wild birds aren't transported and sold, even though the groundwork has been laid with international cooperative agreements.

IV. *New York State Leads the Way*

Within the United States, New York is the only state to adopt a law banning the entry and sale of all wild birds, including many species not yet included on the CITES endangered list. Passed in 1984, the New York statute allows only birds bred in captivity to be sold.

According to the American Federation of Aviculture, eight states (Connecticut, Hawaii, Illinois, Maryland, Massachusetts, Michigan, Pennsylvania, and Washington) have tried, but so far failed to pass similar legislation. In 13 other states—Alaska, Arizona, California, Florida, Minnesota, New Mexico, Ohio, Oregon, South Carolina, South Dakota, Tennessee, Texas, and Utah—even efforts to get the issue on the ballot have been unsuccessful.

Not all these proposals have been as specific as the New York law. Some bills merely provided for restricting the sale of certain species, while others merely called for more studies about the trade in wild birds.

And, while New York State leads the way, there are still glitches. Since the law was passed, the state's protection efforts have been thwarted by citizens who flout the law by purchasing wild birds in other jurisdictions. In a major study of the New York situation, author Laura Simon reports that the pet trade within New York fought the ban even after the law was passed. Their attempt to have the law repealed was defeated in committee by only one vote. Simon adds that the pet trade continues to work against similar legislation in other states and has been largely successful in keeping such initiatives off the ballot.

"Limitations of the New York law underscore the need for federal legislation," says Rupert Cutler, President of Defenders of Wildlife. Only through enactment of a federal law banning all wild bird imports (except to zoos and established captive breeders) can substantial progress be made toward curtailing the abuses in the pet industry. Cutler believes this federal law should require, as a precondition of sale, that vendors band or mark captive-bred birds in a way that would distinguish them immediately from their wild cousins.

However, even with a federal law, much more inspection of imports by JFWAT and their corresponding agencies in other participating nations is needed. Likewise, the full cooperation of pet dealers must be secured, so that they will refuse to sell live wild birds.

V. *The Best Solution*

We need to educate consumers to the cruelty and danger of buying wild birds. If regulators, inspectors, and consumers would insist that pet dealers prove their birds for sale were bred in captivity, the traffic in wild birds would halt and millions of birds from endangered species would be saved.

Unfortunately, pet trade groups and some dealers continue to oppose state and federal laws restricting bird sales to captive-bred birds; these people argue that sales will decline if they can sell only the captive-bred birds.

The facts seem to belie their concern. In New York, pet shop business has actually increased since the state ban was established. By extrapolation, chances are there would be only a slight dip in sales nationwide if federal law required that only birds bred in captivity could be sold.

True, captive-bred birds may be more expensive than birds taken from the wild, but they also make happier pets than their captured wild counterparts. In addition, they can be declared disease-free with a far greater degree of certainty. Not to mention the satisfaction of knowing that by caring for a captive-bred bird, you are contributing to saving the wild bird population throughout the world!

VI. *The Official Policy of the National Humane Education Society*

The Society takes three official positions on this critical issue:

1. Enactment of a federal ban on sales of wild birds is essential.

2. Expanded enforcement by state and federal officials is needed to assure that imports and sales are restricted to captive-bred birds.

3. Consumers should be persuaded through educational efforts to purchase only healthy, captive-bred birds.

All three conditions already exist in Australia; there is no reason why they should not be similarly successful in our country. And there are good reasons why they need to happen in the United States as well as in other countries of the world. If the current legal and illegal, international and domestic trade in wild birds is allowed to continue, the deadly capture, holding, and transport of these creatures will most certainly result in the extinction of some of the world's most beautiful, most precious birds.

Consumers worldwide can play a crucial role in preventing this dreadful outcome by refusing to buy wild birds as pets. Concerned citizens should also write to their state and federal representatives asking them to ban the trade in wild birds. Citizens should urge their local newspapers, magazines, and radio and television stations to run stories on the growing campaign to eliminate the sale of wild birds as pets.

Although it is already illegal in the United States to capture *domestic* wild birds and sell them as pets, we need to extend this law to cover foreign wild birds as well. The only exception to the law should be to permit the humane capture and sale of wild birds to captive breeders and zoos.

To promote better enforcement, many more federal wildlife inspectors are needed to check imports and exports at critical points of entry and exit, so illegal smuggling can be more effectively stopped. Similarly, captive-bred birds should be banded in a special way so that consumers can readily recognized them as legal for sale at pet stores.

In ways such as these, we can preserve the earth's heritage of precious wild birds, which don't deserve to perish at the hands of humans trying to make a buck!

CHAPTER XIV

Do Zoos Care For Wild Animals?

After all the atrocities you've read about in previous chapters—the savage hunting, inhumane breeding, barbarous research experiments, and so forth—you're probably thinking that at least we treat animals in zoos pretty well.

If you believe this, you're partly right and partly wrong. Certainly, most animals in zoos are given better treatment than they are on breeding farms, or in research labs, or left in traps to die. On the other hand, wild animals caught and kept in zoos would hardly consider they had died and gone to heaven.

You'll see what I mean as you read on.

I. *What Are Zoos?*

Zoos are facilities that hold and display wild creatures primarily for recreation and education. They have been with us in many parts of the world for nearly 200 years. Of course, humans have captured and held wild creatures since before recorded history; rulers and prominent citizens often kept large herds of animals as symbols of power and wealth. But these captive flocks were not zoos in the modern-day sense of the word, since they were not usually put on display for all to see.

The first modern-day zoos were founded in Vienna, Madrid, and Paris in the 18th century and in London and

Berlin in the early 19th century. In the United States, Philadelphia and Cincinnati were the first to open zoos in 1870. Today, there are more than 500 zoos in the United States alone, attracting more than 110 million visitors annually. These range from roadside zoos run by hucksters to elaborate parks staffed by trained professionals.

Americans would do well to reflect on the pros and cons of zoos, especially as these might eliminate any needless cruelty and bring about more humane treatment of wild creatures exhibited in such parks. Let's take first the positive points, enumerated by zoo officials and the professional associations representing zoos.

II. *Some Good Points*

Generally, the greater the space zoos can devote to animals, the better. Park-sized zoos are therefore more humane habitats for wild animals than small road-side menageries.

The American Association of Zoological Parks and Aquariums (AAZPA) represents the better-staffed and - run facilities. This professional association offers guidelines on how zoos should be built, managed, and run. The 150 zoos accredited by AAZPA are both recreational and educational and are staffed by teams of professionals which include veterinarians.

Animals placed in zoos run the gamut of mammals, reptiles, amphibians, and birds, some coming from faraway, exotic places. The fact that many zoo animals are not native to the United States is a special attraction to many visitors.

Some officials liken accredited zoos to Noah's ark, although they admit the modern-day facilities are more oriented toward exhibiting and preserving species that are not endangered—whereas, by definition, Noah's species were definitely endangered! However, a recent trend in thinking about zoos focuses on their capacity to rescue and preserve member groups of wild creatures that are endangered in the wild. Zoo officials acknowledge that unless the destruction of vital habitat ceases, many creatures will face extinction in their native habitat.

In this respect, the AAZPA argues that up-to-date zoos are dramatically different from their predecessors. Their innovations are the result of research and improved technology, as well as the desire to serve as conservation havens. As the AAZPA states:

"[We have entered] a new era in which professionally operated zoological institutions have made a commitment to save as many species as possible. Studies of animal behavior in zoos and in the wild played a key role in upgrading the quality of life for captive animals, as well as improving their breeding success."

One major goal of zoos is to secure living specimens from captive flocks rather than from the wild. Reportedly, 80% of mammals displayed in North American zoos are born in captivity. U.S. import documents indicate that less than one tenth of one percent of all wild animals imported into the U.S. are destined for display in zoos.

Given there are more than 110 million visitors each year, zoos are ideal facilities to teach the public about wild species preservation and protection and the enhancement of essential habitat in the wild. The AAZPA considers education an essential component that each zoo must incorporate in its programs in order to win accreditation.

Some zoos maintain exhibits as close as possible to the conditions in the wild which were home for the creatures. Managers incorporate elements from the animal's environment in the wild into their holding areas.

Beyond education, zoos are increasingly involved in saving members of endangered species. By successfully mating the creatures in captivity, populations of some endangered creatures have grown. According to some zoos officials, the ultimate goal is to replenish wild populations where good habitat is protected. To this end, American zoos have already placed some members of endangered species, including the oryx (a wild horse), a tamarin, and one species of parrot, back into the wild.

The AAZPA has also pioneered the Species Survival Plan (SSP), a strategy for the long-term survival of certain endangered animals and a welcome help to zoologists managing these species.

The San Diego and Los Angeles zoos, for example, are at the forefront of efforts to help expand wild populations of California condors that face extinction in the wild. Flocks in the zoos are successfully producing eggs which are hatched in incubators; in the near future, populations of this vulture will again be found in the wild, where a special habitat for them will be permanently protected. The U.S. Fish and Wildlife Service funds and provides vital information to this special project.

Funding is certainly an important consideration. Increasingly, even those zoos that are partially funded by government grants have launched successful fund-raising campaigns to support programs to preserve endangered species in zoos.

Zoo officials today are more successful in caring for animals and allowing for reproduction in captivity because they have at their disposal the many scientific studies conducted by zoologists in the wild. These studies provide reliable information on the needs of animals vital to the proper care of zoo specimens.

With the high cost of acquiring many animals in the wild—including elephants, giraffes, and tigers—carrying out captive reproduction serves the zoos' own interests. Of course, captive breeding also makes possible an increase in populations in zoos without depleting flocks and herds in the wild.

Lastly, since accredited zoos must provide veterinary care for the sick and injured animals, such medical attention coupled with a good diet promotes a longer lifespan for many creatures than is possible in the wild.

III. *The Downside*

Unfortunately, by far the largest number of zoos in the United States do not meet the AAZPA standards and guidelines and are therefore not accredited by the AAZPA. Whether because their pens place animals in unnecessarily restricted confinement, or because zookeepers provide insufficient association with other creatures, or because they fail to offer proper nutrition and veterinary care—many facilities need to be upgraded in order to qualify as humane facilities.

Key factors to be considered are matching the exhibited animals with proper temperature, rainfall, and terrain conditions. Tropical animals placed in less temperate areas should be given smaller quarters to protect them from the cold winter. Grazing animals must be allowed to browse in natural-like settings where climate is not a hindering factor. Polar bears can suffer greatly in zoos that are very warm in summer or warm all year long.

Since exotic creatures are often preferred by zoo managers and keepers because of their popularity with visitors, a frequent objection at many unaccredited zoos is that they fail to properly select and account for climate, and they provide inadequate treatment and poor diets.

By far the most serious objection to many zoos is confinement. Creatures such as elephants and other large mammals, large reptiles, and even large birds are cared for most of the time in small areas which greatly restrict movement. Confinement often leads to serious behavioral disorders that keep the creatures from making a healthy adjustment to their lives in captivity.

Creatures are not machines that can be manipulated freely. Like humans, animals are used to freedom of movement. Indeed, many creatures in the wild prefer migrating rather than adjusting to inhospitable climatic conditions. But in zoos, despite whatever drive or need they may have for seasonal or other types of mass movement, creatures are denied such freedom.

The main role most zoos carry out is recreation. People are encouraged to visit these parks to view rare, unusual creatures and see how they behave. Because of their limited space in cages or restricted external quarters, however, animals seldom reveal the true natural behavior they would exhibit in the wild.

Zoos have a captive audience of 110 million people a year, so they should provide a perfect place to educate the public about animal needs and preferences. Actually, however, except for a token blurb hung here and there near the animals' pens explaining the animal's habitat, most people come away in complete ignorance of how vital habitat and other natural conditions are for animals in the wild. So it's not surprising that, rather than acquiring a respect for wild creatures in their natural habitat, people leave zoos thinking that animals are cute little robots who perform freely and naturally in front of the public.

As for zoos functioning like Noah's ark, exhibiting facilities in many instances fail in this respect. True, some members of endangered species are surviving in zoos, but they would probably not make it if they were returned to the wild, because they have become too dependent on humans in the meantime. They are like hothouse creatures incapable of fending and providing for themselves in the wild. So, when breeding animals in captivity, extra care should be taken to prevent a dependence on people for sustenance—something most of the zoos cannot guarantee.

While the larger zoos have the above-mentioned drawbacks, there is virtually no justification for the typical roadside zoo, whose only purpose is to make money by having visitors pay for admission. Even if it were granted that zoos should charge a fee for viewing, the issue of how this money is used is a legitimate concern. Roadside zoo owners too often just pocket the money; in the larger, more humane zoos, on the other hand, funds are primarily spent on improving the conditions of the animals being displayed.

Many zoos allow creatures to mate and give birth to offspring far beyond a reasonable number needed for exhibition. Because many people think it is "cute" to witness the behavior of the young specimens, zoo managers often encourage these births only to keep the public satisfied. And many creatures bred in captivity face a dubious existence. They are often put on the auction block, and buyers are not asked what their intentions are with regard to these creatures. And those which are not sold are often confined to areas of the zoo that the public is not invited to see.

IV. *The Official Policy of the National Humane Education Society*

Because so many zoos have not yet won accreditation by the AAZPA, it is more than likely that many animals in captivity are being subjected to inhumane conditions. Our Society therefore feels the following conditions should be met before zoos are allowed to exhibit wild creatures:

1. Zoos must meet stringent nutrition, veterinary care, and professional staff requirements to be allowed to operate.

2. Zoos should charge admission fees or otherwise obtain financial support to run the parks humanely.

3. Zoo managers should seek, as far as possible, to replicate the habitats and climatic conditions the wild animals were originally used to. Polar bears exhibited in Florida and alligators in Boston will suffer from

inhospitable climate unless they are given the proper quarters. Where animals' requirements cannot be accommodated, they should not be kept in zoos.

4. Zoos should have materials and advisors on hand to teach people about the ecology and conservation of creatures in the wild. In this way, young people can be shown how to acquire healthy respect for animal lives in all their diversity.

5. Zoos can be a part of organized professional efforts to save species from extinction by captive breeding and placing the newly born at a suitable age into the wild where habitats suitable for animals are protected.

6. On the other hand, indiscriminate breeding merely to exhibit the new-born creatures should cease. Captive breeding should be carried out only in numbers that can be cared for and humanely exhibited throughout the country.

7. Because roadside zoos operate solely to make money for owners and are therefore inhumane, they should be abolished.

8. Park-sized zoos can serve a legitimate purpose in showing wild creatures to advantage for recreation. To do so, though, education should come before recreation as the major reason for permitting zoos to exist.

V. *Conclusion*

Zoos, more than any other form of recreation, offer ideal opportunities to teach the importance of habitat protection for members of the species existing in the wild. Young people coming to zoos should be properly instructed concerning animal life, so they carry away healthy impressions about the needs of creatures. All visitors should be encouraged to reject the notion that animals are robots or automatons put on earth only to serve as a source of recreation for people. All creatures have the right to live freely and purposefully regardless of where they are found.

CONCLUSION

This book has addressed 14 of the most important issues in the humane field and presented the official position of The National Humane Education Society relative to each. As president of the Society, I appreciate and take pride in being chosen to share this work as part of our ongoing humane education effort.

The National Humane Education Society's principal mission is to foster a sentiment of kindness to animals in children and adults. I hope the information contained in this work will do much towards that end.

Most certainly, the topics addressed in this book have often been weighty; however, they are not meant to present positions which the reader should adopt ready-made. It is assumed that the individual will formulate his or her opinions based on a personal value system. Anyone who gives these matters much thought will find themselves struggling to develop a personal ethic to guide their decisions about the care and treatment of animals across these areas of concern.

To the extent this book helps to guide the reader through the nooks and crannies of one's own experiences and character, I believe it has served its purpose well. After all, that is the beginning from which humane care will spring.

—Anna C. Briggs